BARN STORIES

BARN STORIES

REFLECTIONS FROM A SARATOGA COUNTY HORSE FARM

MARY CUFFE PEREZ

NORTH COUNTRY BOOKS, INC.
UTICA, NEW YORK

The stories in this book are creative nonfiction based upon real experiences.
People's names have been changed, but most horses' names have not.
Some of the characters are composites and some are fictionalized.

ISBN 978-1-59531-057-6

Design by Zach Steffen & Rob Igoe, Jr.

Library of Congress Cataloging-in-Publication Data

Names: Cuffe-Perez, Mary, 1946- , author.
Title: Barn stories : stories from a Saratoga County horse farm / by Mary
    Cuffe Perez.
Description: Utica, New York : North Country Books, 2017.
Identifiers: LCCN 2017036017 | ISBN 9781595310576 (alk. paper)
Subjects: LCSH: Horse boarding facilities--New York (State)--Saratoga
    County--Anecdotes.. | Horses--New York (State)--Saratoga
    County--Anecdotes. | Horsemen and horsewomen--New York (State)--Saratoga
    County--Anecdotes.
Classification: LCC SF285.375.U6 C84 2017 | DDC 636.1009747/48--dc23
LC record available at https://lccn.loc.gov/2017036017

North Country Books, Inc.
220 Lafayette Street
Utica, New York 13502
www.northcountrybooks.com

In memory of Marcia

CONTENTS

INTRODUCTION

I HAVE BEEN INTRIGUED BY OLD BARNS since I was five years old, when my grandmother took me to the neighboring farm to see the new kittens born in the loft. Ever since, barns have been places of discovery for me—as liable to produce a litter of kittens as the they are clues to the many lives that once passed through them.

Barns are sheltering places. That is true whether they are full of cattle or horses—with fresh cut hay in the loft—or abandoned, harboring cats, owls, and spiders. Even, I suspect, a ghost or two.

The barn in this collection began accumulating its stories long before I came along. It was built in the late eighteenth century and is situated in the rural community of Galway, New York, where I live. I have taken care of the horses boarded at the farm for over fifteen years, and kept my own horse, Angel, there. The stories included in this book are based upon real experiences I have had over the years.

Life at the barn is never static. It flows with the tides of light that sweep across the floorboards, with the cycle of seasons, with the kids and adults who slide open those heavy front doors, with cats, with wildlife, and with horses. Some pass through in the blink of an eye, others stay a lifetime.

Each has left something of themselves to become part of the barn's life and timelessness—the barn's stories.

THE FIFTH SEASON

I CALL THE GIANT SUGAR MAPLE that tops the Rumsley drive "Shoog"—
short for "Shoogah." That's how my Aunt Sabra used to pronounce "sugar,"
a term of affection down South. I sure have affection for the old maple. It's
older than the farmhouse and barn, and has held up its piece of sky since
before the first Scottish settlers slapped down their claim to this corner of
Saratoga County. Shoog is always last to lose its leaves, but last night's rain
broke autumn down like a road show.

There is no light on in the kitchen of the farm house. Only a thin tail of
smoke rises from the chimney in the still air. Arvis is probably next to the
stove, sucking on his tobacco-less pipe, sipping coffee. He's up most days
by five. Come winter, he'll catch me as I walk up to the barn and call out
the temperature. Just so I know it's twenty below, rather than the fifteen
below everywhere else. For some reason, it's always coldest on this farm.
For some reason, Arvis likes to remind me of that.

As I walk up the long slope to the barn, I feel a hitch of worry. Only two
horses are waiting at the fence.

The horses know the pitch of my car's engine and have come from the
front pasture, drawn away from the few apples that remain on the low
branches of the apple trees in the hedgerow. There are just three mares
now—Angel, my Arabian; Trixster, Marilyn's quarter horse; and Victoria,
a Thoroughbred cross and the only boarder. Without her, there would be
nothing to call this farm a business. Victoria must still be making her way
in from the pasture. The oldest and frailest of the three, she may not make

it through another winter.

If Marilyn were here, she would announce with histrionic finality that the riding season was done. She made this statement every year at this time as if ending the riding season was a conspiracy of the Left. But we seldom rode into November, anyway, except for that bewildering winter two years ago. The seasons didn't change that year, but lapsed into a fifth season that hung suspended between fall and winter. Mid-January Marilyn and I rode through Slovak's fields, but it felt all wrong. The fields, which should have been tucked under a good foot of snow, were bare and sodden. That was our last ride together.

This year, winter will not falter. The horses' coats are bristling. The little garden I keep on the south side of the barn is shorn to a few collard greens. Last night's freezing rain has brought us down to what has been—the barn, the coming of winter, the horses. Beyond that, there's no telling. Since Marilyn's death last spring, it feels as though we are in a fifth season again, waiting for whatever the next thing will be. There's nothing to hold Arvis to a 180-acre farm that supports just three horses. Since I've known him, he's talked about moving to the coast of Maine where he and Marilyn spent their summers. Everyone keeps asking me when he's going to sell. "I don't know," I tell them. "I just take care of the horses."

Victoria finally joins the other two horses at the fence, completing my landscape of care. They are three black, cut-out figures against the sky, the outline of their heads and necks and the alertness of ears their own geography. They keen in my direction. Angel whinnies softly. It is a call that says *feed me*, but it says more too. At least, I take it as such. It says we are in this together—this foundering horse farm, the coming winter, the routine that binds us. A black cat, hungry too, slips out of the stone foundation and disappears under the barn doors ahead of me. Anything can slip into this old barn— wind, stray cats, blown snow. From the road it looks like its own mountain, but the Rumsley barn is more vision than substance. Nothing is straight, true, or secure. You would not think it could keep anything. But it does.

Angel calls again, this time with more insistence. She is reminding me of what is here and now, the necessity of getting on with it. I slide open the barn doors. The horses, on cue, turn to be let in.

THE HORSE BUSINESS

"THE HORSE BUSINESS is a stopper yanked out of a drain," Arvis used to say, so I was surprised he agreed to take on the horse-boarding business after Marilyn's death. Most folks around here were surprised he didn't sell the farm outright. It was well known that it was her love and his burden. After his retirement, eleven years ago, there was no escape from the fence mending, mowing of fields, and shoring up of the old barn. Arvis was much better adapted to piloting his little fishing skiff off the coast of Maine than bucking over the fields in a 1964 incontinent tractor. He is even allergic to horsehair and hay. But Marilyn would have her horses.

Marilyn was a horsewoman all her life, and marrying Arvis, who had no use for anything on the hoof, didn't change that. Buying the farm over his common sense objections took her years of bargaining and battling, and the battle was still at full pitch by the time I came on the scene thirty years later. It boosted Marilyn's cause that their daughter, Nancy, shared her mother's love for horses and was riding before her feet could reach the stirrups. The tack room is decorated with ribbons Marilyn and Nancy won during the years they both competed in horse shows throughout the Northeast in jumping and dressage class. After retiring from competition, Marilyn turned her enormous energies to designing and constructing a cross-country course on the farm to host Pony Club competitions. The remnants of the course still wind through the fields and forests—tire jumps, stone fences, precipitous slopes plunging to stream crossings.

By the time I met Marilyn she called herself a casual rider and operated a small breeding business at the farm. She was continually arming herself with whatever argument she could invent to defend the profitability of her horse-breeding program against Arvis' Excel charts that proved otherwise. But, as I discovered long ago with the pair of them, nothing really added up.

From outward appearances, the Rumsleys lived in a state of verbal barrage. Their customary manner of addressing one another was long distance, lofting commands and refutations across fields at one another. Often caught between volleys, I learned to duck and go about my business. Of the two, Marilyn's voice was by far the greater weapon. I would be just sliding open the barn doors, getting ready for an afternoon ride or to do chores, when *Mary!*, hurtled from the raised kitchen window half an acre downwind, would strike with enough force to scare the breath out of me. I never quite got used to it.

Reviving the farm as a business was at least a posturing of pragmatism for Arvis. Until he decided to sell, boarding horses would be a good tax write-off. But what really held him to the farm was Marilyn—her ghost, her echo. For my part, managing the business would give me a place to keep Angel and a little extra money from the boarding fees. That was the short version, anyway.

To fill the six stalls in the barn, I thought I'd tack up a "Horse Boarding" sign in the village feed store with a few descriptive phrases, post an ad on Craigslist, and wait for my cell phone to ring. It did, but not with grounded inquiries. Instead, I became entangled in personal dramas of betrayals, evictions, assaults, and the gamut of tragedies, all loosely wrapped around the ownership of a horse in some way or another. "Can you hold a place for my horse?" one person inquired. "I just have to wait for the owner to die."

There were promises, excuses, an expectation that "things would work out," a date and time set for potential boarders to view the farm. Not one of them showed. The summer wore on without the prospect of a single

The tools of that time are bolted onto the outside wall of the tack room or hung from the cross beams, serving only as conversation pieces today — wooden hay rakes, flails, a four-finger bow cradle for hand-cutting grain and hay, bow ax, buck saw, augers, wooden mallets, and other forged tools that are put to no purpose now. These curious, hand-crafted implements form a kind of language, as if of a lost civilization.

The original barn was about half the size of the barn that stands today. There were no stalls; draft horses and other livestock were sheltered in the understory of the barn, long since boarded up, and hay and grain were piled in two side bays. Sometime in the mid-eighteen hundreds, the barn was converted to keep dairy cattle and store larger quantities of hay. The south walls and their sliding doors came down at that time, and a new section was added on for stanchions with a hay mow above. In this new configuration, hay was lifted from the wagons by a rope and pulley system supported from the ridgepole and attached to a hay hook that lifted bundles of loose hay into the mow. The basketball-sized pulley used in this operation still hangs from the ridgepole today. By the middle of the nineteenth century, the small farm dairy business could no longer compete with larger, more mechanized operations, and the threshing barn turned cow barn became a horse barn, with stalls replacing stanchions. When the Rumsleys bought the place in the 1960s, they added a tack room to the west bay and another run-in shed on the east side of the barn.

The barn today speaks mostly of horses, but the other stories are there too, a layer or two deep.

A horse whisperer once told me that horses are tuned to "spirits." They see and hear several dimensions deep, she said, while humans function in the shallows of what their senses reveal. If that is true, the horses have lots of company in this barn. Looking up along those hand- chinked beams to the ceiling above and the stream of light issuing from the window at the peak, you feel the ripple of time — the rumble of wagons and tractors over the wide oaken boards of the main bay, the heat of livestock, the drum of hooves and boots, the wagonloads of hay hoisted into the mow, the buckwheat threshed on the barn floor, the winnowed seed rising into the same shaft of light I stand in.

Through the changes in times and purpose, the barn has harbored all manner of wildlife: the swallows that build their nests in the joists; the brown bats that hang from the ridgepole; the owls that dip in through the gaps in the barn siding in search of mice; the spiders with webs swinging like phantom udders from windows and corners; the cats crouched in the mow, under floor boards, behind tack trunks; the mice and skunks and raccoons and even fox that ease through the stone foundation to take shelter in the understory. All the life this one place holds.

On winter days when wind slices through the siding, snow sweeps across the wide floor boards, and the beams and doors groan their lamentations, you might think only ghosts live here now. But rattle the pie tins and the cats dart down from the mow; then, open the back doors and call the horses in. They'll be close by. It's winter. They're hungry and impatient. Feel the barn expand as they enter, stomping and blowing, steam rising from their backs, their muzzles wet, dark eyes lit with the fire of life.

ROBERT KELSO'S SADDLE

OLD BARNS ARE NEVER QUITE ABANDONED. What passes through, passes incompletely. All they have sheltered, harbored, stored leave something of themselves behind. When I enter an old barn today, I feel the presence of what was as strongly as what is, like someone I've known all my life. I see more than whom they have become, but also what they've left behind.

I was five-years-old when I entered my first barn, a Pennsylvania bank barn, the summer we lived with my grandparents. My grandfather had sold off his herd years before, and the old barn had to be in decline by then. But I remember it as a radiant, white vessel cresting the hillside, dominating the landscape. Its grandiosity spoke of a time when barns were revered— the three-story loftiness, the overhang of the fore bay, and the elegant little cupolas on either end, the purpose of which I re-imagined many times over. But it was the interior of the barn that gathered me in and never completely let me go.

No radiance there. The only light yearned through glaucous windows and missing sideboards. The draft that welled up through the floorboards was the cold breath of inner earth carrying with it the loam of long-aged manure from the underground bay. It raised a fine dust that hung in the air and coated beams and rafters. The hay mow, another story high, was piled with broken hay bales, grayed with mold and sour with rot. Above, much higher, a colony of brown bats clustered at the ridgepole. From everywhere, but nowhere visible, scratching, scurrying, and the seep of furtive, submerged voices. Mice, perhaps. Perhaps.

I should have been terrified, but instead I was drawn deeper. An intriguing shape straddled a sawhorse in the far corner of the barn. I hopped over gaps in the floorboards, eyeing the black depths below, and squeezed past cow stanchions. It was a saddle, I knew, even before I slid aside the gray woolen blanket that covered it. I stood with the tattered blanket crumbling in my hand, awed by my discovery. I ran my palm over the arch of the pommel, the sweep of cantle, knowing nothing of the parts of a saddle, yet feeling the actions they were crafted to. Rosettes of mildew bloomed on the flaps and the seat was coated with a green patina of mold, but rubbing my fingers into the deep seat recalled the luster. Like blowing on embers.

My grandfather called it an Australian stock saddle. It had belonged to my great-grandfather, Robert Kelso, a man no one seemed to know very much about. Or so it seemed. My pious and proudly sober grandfather clearly disapproved of his father, a flamboyant Scotsman fatally fond of horses and single malt scotch. I later learned that Robert Kelso had left or been driven from his homeland in Scotland as a very young man for reasons left dangling in family history. He had been a horse trader, carpenter, and itinerant electrician until he finally married and settled in Pennsylvania to become a failed farmer. Among the few graces my grandfather allowed him was that he was a fine builder of barns and a great storyteller, though no one today remembers his stories.

By the time I came along there was little left to find him by—just a few black-and-white photographs, taken from a distance, and the words others used to define him. But even at five-years-old, I knew he had been someone else too, and the saddle connected us.

He had built the barn and the barn remembered. Among the stanchions, piles of lumber, motor parts, coils of electrical wire, and sagging cardboard boxes of rusted nails, I searched for clues to Robert Kelso. The few I found were enough to build a vision upon—cribbed boards from the stall where he kept his last horse, a curry comb, a hoof pick, a dirt- and sweat-encrusted saddle pad with red horse hairs still clinging to it. And, of course, the saddle. The stitching like code beneath my fingers, the live smell of horse. Static as it was, it spoke of energy and flight. Horse and rider. I imagined it spoke the same language to Robert Kelso.

After we moved from Pennsylvania to Washington State, I never entered that barn again. My grandfather died soon after and the farm was sold. I have often wondered what happened to Robert Kelso's saddle. But whatever its fate, I still know where to find it.

PATHS OUT TO PASTURE

WHEN I WAS ELEVEN YEARS OLD, the fantasies that had fluttered around in my head about horses settled into the solid determination to own one. I had an ally in my best friend, Norma Roger. She lived right next door and horses were all we ever talked about. We spent hours plotting ways to earn enough money to buy a horse, what color it would be and what we would name it, leaving other details—such as where to stable it and how to feed it—to sort themselves out later. We lived in stilt-supported houses on a wooded hillside that sloped steeply down to Puget Sound. No land for horses, no money for boarding horses. Norma figured this out before I did. It became a lonely battle trying to hold onto that dream, and eventually, I let it go.

When my husband, Ken, and I moved to the rural town of Galway in Upstate New York, that eleven-year-old popped up again. Horses were everywhere. Just two miles from our house there were three horse farms where Hermance Road, the road we live on, intersected with Parkis Mills Road. The Rumsley farm was another mile left on Parkis Mills. I could not pass the farm without stopping. I came to know the sweep of pasture, the hedgerows, the barn on the hill, the rim of forest as you know a half-remembered dream—intensely, vividly, but without anything solid to pin it to. Sometimes as I stood watching them over the fence, the horses would turn from their grazing to consider me briefly, as if trying to remember too.

If I rode my bike by the farm at the right time, I'd catch sight of a far-away figure at the back door of the barn calling to the horses in a voice so commanding it could have summoned troops. She would wave at me and

I waved back. I'd watch until the last horse was in, the door closed.

One day, the distant figure confronted me at the roadside. She was replacing a fence rail, she said, but I had an inkling she had been waiting for me. Two of the horses had followed her to the fence, as if I was a curiosity they were finally brave enough to investigate. I don't remember our conversation exactly, more the impression Marilyn made upon me. She was small, blond, abrupt. It must have been the bright June air that made her seem to be bristling with static, the light snapping off everything—her eyes and cheeks, and her hair as it blew around, mixed with the horses' manes. After introductions, she came to the point: "Do you want to take a look around the farm?"

And I was caught like a fly in amber.

She invited me to come on a ride with her, and before the summer was out, I was a regular at the farm, helping with barn chores in exchange for riding Lizzie, one of Marilyn's quiet and patient brood mares. Marilyn taught me the routine of the barn, its many quirks and conditions, and just about everything I know about horses that horses didn't teach me directly. By that fall, she'd helped me realize that latent dream: a horse of my own. To offset the cost of boarding Angel at the Rumsleys' barn, I took care of all the horses whenever Marilyn and Arvis were away.

Now that Marilyn is gone, I come twice a day, every day.

When the horses have been let out of the barn after their evening feeding, I often stand and watch as the last light of the day follows the rhythmic swing of their gait out to pasture. The paths they have worn are carved as deeply into the earth as the routine of coming here is carved into me. I've never been so committed to anything. I don't know if it is the love of horses or the loss of a friend or the place itself that holds me. Maybe it's just the way the sun touches everything with a kind of tenderness as it leaves—horses, fields, forest, sky, me—as if to set us all in place.

THE LAST HORSE

TRIXSTER WAS MARILYN'S LAST HORSE—a roan quarter horse mare, quiet and small, to accommodate the limitations of arthritis. Before Trixster, there was a lifetime of horses: magnificent and athletic Trakehners, Hanoverians, Morgans, and Thoroughbreds; jumpers, prancers, eventers, racers, driving horses, trail horses. I come upon their names on plaques and halters, turnout blankets and brushes tucked in trunks or in corners of the barn. Shadow Dancer, Magic, Lizzie, Serendipity, Foxy Lady, Maisy, Maya.

Marilyn was a fearless rider, even when I knew her, long after the equestrian feats of her youth. My perspective, during our rides, was usually from behind. I can still see Maya, Marilyn's riding horse before Trixster, taking the McClellan's hill ahead of me—the horse's chestnut rump and black flag of tail and Marilyn's pants seat raised just off the saddle as she leaned into the gallop up the long flank of hill to the bank of white pines at the top. This was always our first ride of the season, just after the snow was off the fields. Or early summer, through wooded trails that wound along the Gloweegie just as dark was coming on, and I could only make out the tan seat of Marilyn's riding breeches in front of me. Or best of all, through Slovak's after the second cutting of hay, when we flew over those undulating fields as if there was no possibility of a woodchuck hole, a tractor rut, or the startle of wild turkeys to impede our flight.

For Marilyn, these were tame rides. In her youth she rode cross-country, clearing stone walls and streams, galloping through open fields, down and up embankments. She once told me that the first horse she owned as a girl growing up on the Massachusetts coast was a Thoroughbred stallion so hot he could only be stopped by riding him into the surf.

There is no name plaque for that stallion here in this barn. He was part of her life before she moved to Galway with Arvis. The horses that came after and the uses they were put to are part of this barn's accumulated history, as are a driving cart, a carriage with a red velvet seat, and a cutter that claim the entire east bay of the barn. The Rumsley years fill the tack room with large wooden trunks of harnesses, bridles, halters, leads, riding crops, grooming utensils, wraps, and ointments. Saddles for jumping, dressage, and trail riding remain at rest on saddle trees along one wall. Everywhere the eye lands are ribbons from shows and cross-country events. Stakes with red flags attached, once used to mark the cross-country trails that ran through the farm, are stacked at one end of the hay mow.

The layers of history in this barn are as thick as the dust. But Marilyn's story is so recent it hasn't yet settled into history. She lives on the air, still snapping and sparking. I brace for the jolt of her voice each time I slide open the impossibly heavy barn doors, and often find myself about to ask for her consultation—is it time to call the farrier? How long do you think the grass will hold? How long should I keep the mares separated from the geldings? Do you think I should blanket tonight? And I still expect she's watching censoriously as I measure out the grain, throw hay to the horses, or muck out the stalls. The cats, always startled away when she entered the barn, still peek down from the hay mow to make sure she isn't there before drifting down for their food. And I'm sure when the horses look up suddenly, prick their ears and flare their nostrils, it's Marilyn. Right over my shoulder.

AMONGOOSEAMONGUS

MONGOOSE—a shortened version of her racing name—turned out to be an apt handle for the new boarder, the first after a summer-long search. The filly was not at all what I was hoping for. She was small for a Thoroughbred at just over 15 hands, but it seemed, as I watched her unload from the trailer, that there were at least three horses compressed within her. Her owner, Jaycee, was talking to me, but I didn't catch a word. I was distracted by an optical illusion—the lead line connecting Jaycee to the thoroughbred was barely taut, yet the horse appeared to be levitating. Jaycee was probably telling me how to take charge—her mantra. Standing there dangling the lead line like it was the handle of a designer pocketbook, she looked like being in charge came pretty easily to her.

I have to admit, I was intimidated by Jaycee. She was a lot like her horse. I felt myself blown backwards when Jaycee approached. Her gestures and movements were quick and deliberate; handy, I guess, for dealing with flighty thoroughbreds. Her voice was a ground-shaking baritone. When she issued a command, the birds fell silent. She spoke so fast in a Long Island accent that I could hardly snatch a word from a sentence.

"She'll come down." She gave a sharp yank of the lead line. "Just let her know you're the boss," she said as she led Mongoose into the paddock, twirling the end of the lead rope. When the filly caught sight of the three horses grazing in the pasture, Jaycee smacked her with a command and a tug of the lead line. The horse snorted once and dropped her head, half her attention angled toward the other horses.

While Jaycee stood there talking to me about what I probably should have been listening to, Mongoose seemed to swallow the landscape. She was like a dark, impenetrable forest that you are afraid to enter, but are irresistibly drawn to. Her black eyes flashed run, run, run. I couldn't look away from her.

Mongoose was a "rescue," Jaycee explained, though I doubt Mongoose realized that. Jaycee had been the horse's trainer and bought her owners out when they made the decision to put her down after a knee injury ended her racing career. But Mongoose wasn't the usual rescue story. Jaycee hadn't taken over ownership of the Thoroughbred for the sake of a Disney-type ending. Mongoose had aristocratic bloodlines. Her sire was Unbridled, Horse of the Year in 1999. She would be bred to a proven stallion in hopes of producing a foal for the yearling sales in Saratoga. Watching the filly gather like a storm at sea, it was impossible to attach the phrase "put down" to the ascending life force that was Mongoose.

"Just don't back down," Jaycee said at the end of another rapid-fire, run-on sentence. I must have missed what came before it, because now the lead line was in my hand and Jaycee was turning to go. Then gone. She moved so fast, I wished I could rewind. I stood there with run-run-run at the end of the lead line.

The usual "settling in" procedure at the farm was to keep new arrivals separated from the other horses for a day or two to allow them time to make their introductions safely over the fence—lay out their conditions, so to speak—before they were all turned out together. But as soon as I unclipped the lead line from the filly's halter, I knew I had lost all say.

Mongoose exploded. I flattened myself against the side of the barn as she hit the ground and stormed the fence like it was the inside rail of Saratoga Racetrack. She spun out when she reached the end and charged back again. When she surged up against the fence rails, I knew she would either break through or jump them. I'd have to skip introductions.

But I couldn't capitulate entirely, or I would lose all hope of control. I had to show I was in charge, as Jaycee said. Or at least *there*. I would lead her into the pasture.

She skidded to a stop when she saw me approach with the lead line. Her head flew up, eyes wide with excitement, ears flicking. She was either going to run right past me or through me. To my heart-thumping surprise, she went stone still. I reached out, touched her shoulder, then her neck, and finally clipped the lead line to her halter. "There's a girl," I squeaked. She looked past me. Her training had turned her into a kind of racing machine, responding to cues, but not to the person behind them. She was a horse at the starting gate.

Blessedly, the lead line held some kind of magic. As long as she was clipped to it, she was controlled, but as soon as I opened the gate and unclipped her, all three of those horses stuffed inside broke loose. I held my breath as she bolted toward the others and then skidded to a stop just feet in front of them. The three stood motionless, every angle of their bodies pointed at the newcomer. Mongoose seemed not to know what to do next. She blew, pawed the ground, nickered, shook her head. No response from the others. She lowered her head, surrendering her proud profile, and approached slowly.

Angel flattened her ears and charged, set on establishing her dominance in the little herd of mares. Mongoose jumped aside. Angel charged again. This time, the other two horses, catching on now, joined in.

It wasn't much of a chase. Mongoose, neck arched, ears pricked, tail a high-flying flag, seemed amused, then delighted by the attention. She pranced and hopped in a parody of a lamb's gambol in widening circles around the other horses. The three mares lurched and lunged after her, unable to close any distance. Victoria, the oldest and frailest, gave up the chase first; then Angel, realizing she'd been made a fool of, and finally Trixster, who would have liked to play a little longer.

Angel and Victoria stood blowing their outrage into the air as Mongoose continued to romp around them. Trixster was in awe. After a while, all three turned their rumps to the newcomer and began to graze. Mongoose continued to hop and prance, but it was clear the others were done with the chase. She stopped and called to them, but they ignored her splendidly.

Perhaps out of frustration, or maybe just to show off, Mongoose went up on her back legs and shot into full gallop. She rumbled into the distance, the drum of hooves diminishing to patters, then silence, as she reached the end of the five-acre field, thundering again as she galloped back. She slid to a halt in front of the other horses, head and tail high, blowing furiously. Then she turned and did it all over again.

The little group of horses and I had taken notice. We had a Mongoose among us.

FOALS, THE FOLLY OF

HIGH SUMMER. The foals born in late April are old enough to be cocky. Marilyn is exceptionally proud of these two—a bay filly with a white blaze and three white stockings, and a big-boned gray colt. She has already lined up buyers for them once they're weaned. But for this brief time, before their wills are bent to a purpose, they are that mercurial being, a foal. No more a horse than a child is an adult. Their hooves barely touch the ground as they fly out the barn's back door ahead of their burdened mothers and gallop to the far end of the front pasture without a look back. The two mares have already dismissed them and buried their muzzles in orchard grass.

I'm helping Marilyn with morning chores so we can go riding afterwards, but I'm too charmed by the foals to do anything but stand at the back door and watch them buck and kick and ram into one another. Suddenly, they pull up short. Something in the front pasture has drawn their attention taut.

I can't see what it is until a head and neck periscope above the grasses— the resident wild turkey clan, two or three families that prowl the pasture for grasshoppers, grubs, and seed heads. Four hens are in the lead and another takes up the flank, shepherding a couple dozen poults between.

Marilyn joins me at the back door. "What are those babies up to?" she asks. Foal watching is one of our favorite activities. We could stand there for half an hour with hardly a word passing between us. The less said the better. Our sanctuary of common ground is horses.

"The colt's got good bone," Marilyn observes. The foals, usually all loops and twirls and flying legs, have gone still as statues.

"But the filly's a nicer mover," I add.

"That's Saffire!" Marilyn is pleased that her choice of sire has produced another foal that has lived up to its breeding.

The two are not concerned with their breeding or what their purpose will be, or anything beyond this brilliant morning in late June paraded through by a flock of aliens. The turkeys aren't concerned, either, not yet anyway. Turkeys have shared this pasture through generations of horses. Horses, they know, are alarmists, but will accept almost anything once it becomes an established part of the landscape.

For the foals, their landscape is still in flux. There are no limits, no routines, no paths out to pasture. Each day their world expands farther beyond their mothers' sides, from the cavernous barn with its creaking, thumping, and rumbling to the big open sky of the pasture, that blowing, gushing world of sounds and shapes, where very little can be counted on to stay in place; where each invention the world comes up with must be added to their known landscape, chronicled as either something to run from, investigate, or have fun with.

The week before, Marilyn and I had watched from the same spot as deer stepped into the young ones' world for the first time. While the other horses did not even raise their heads to acknowledge the deer, the foals approached with heads lowered like hunting dogs, stalking, stopping as the deer stopped. There was a brief standoff before the deer lost interest and trotted off across the pasture without bothering to hoist a flag. The foals must have thought they had something to do with it. They galloped a few victory laps around one another before bounding back to their mothers.

Wild turkeys are not as big as deer, but a far stranger "something." Their thrusting, arrow-shaped heads and clacking noises unsettle the colt. He decides they belong to the "something to run away from" category and gallops back to his mother's side. The filly decides they are "something fun."

She takes a step forward, tentatively following the turkey procession.

"She's a bold one." Marilyn says. "The colt has more sense." But I notice the little gleam of approval in her eye.

The hens sound the alarms, a series of putt-putt utterances that scatter the poults through the grasses. The filly, momentarily baffled by the evacuation, regroups and hops after the hens. She is about to learn a humbling lesson: turkeys don't play.

From our perspective, back at the barn, it could be a scene on the Serengeti—wing flapping, raucous clacking, and somewhere beneath the feathered melee, the filly. The mares look on with mild interest as the filly emerges, bucks off a turkey, and gallops free.

Safely gathered within her own, the filly stares after the turkeys, which have summoned their young from hiding with high-pitched yelps and resumed their procession across the field as if the little drama that had just played out had nothing to do with them. The filly blows and stomps the last word as she watches them disappear into the hedgerow.

"That will teach her!" Marilyn says as she turns to go back to her chores.

But of course we both hope it doesn't.

ARCHIE AND VIENTO

MARILYN HAD ALWAYS ASSERTED that mixing mares with geldings was inviting trouble, but there were two stalls to fill and Lyla was a prospective boarder with two five-year-old geldings. She'd lost her own Thoroughbred horse farm to circumstances involving a "barbarous" ex-husband who, she claimed, duped her out of everything except the two geldings and a trust fund. It couldn't have been hard to dupe Lyla. She appeared half conscious most of the time. I wasn't sure she was always sober, but decided to attribute her haziness to Arvis' conviction that horse people are all a little crazy.

So there we stood that late August afternoon as Viento and Archie stormed the boundaries of their new home. Neither had ever known turnout beyond the confines of a paddock, and they raced one another the perimeter of the front pasture at a lethal gallop. Watching them, it occurred to me just how imaginary the fencing was. Lyla, swaying in high-heeled sandals, was unconcerned. She absently dropped her cigarette butt in the water tank as she rattled off feeding instructions for her horses. Archie, a 17-hand bay, was an ex-racehorse that Lyla had picked up "for a song" and planned to sell to one of her track connections as a lead pony. "Pony" didn't apply to Archie at all. Nor did Thoroughbred. He looked like he was better suited to the plow. Viento, a striking dapple-gray Trekaner-Thoroughbred cross, was her riding horse.

"*Your* riding horse?" I asked, unable to conceal my astonishment. Lyla had opened her mouth to reply when the horses, rounding the corner of the barn, barreled down upon us.

I ducked beside the water tank as Lyla vanished in an avalanche of lathered up horse flesh, then reappeared, still intact, as the geldings snorted, farted, and bolted away. "He's five-gaited," she resumed, lifting her hand to her mouth and realizing she no longer held a cigarette.

We watched as the horses circled the pasture for the third time. The four mares, still brooding about being confined to the back pasture, ambled over to the gate that separated them from the front pasture. They had turned their rumps to the two geldings the moment they arrived, but now curiosity overtook scorn. All four stood alertly watching the pair, their ears flicking back and forth. Even Mongoose seemed disdainful of such unnecessary exertions on such a perfect late-summer day. There were loaded apple trees in the hedgerow and an afternoon of grazing to do. Angel gave a snort of disgust and walked away. Trixster, Mongoose, and Victoria followed.

After Lyla left, I returned to check on the horses. The boys had finally run themselves out. Archie was absorbed in earnest grazing. Viento, however, was performing. He floated in a high-stepping prance back and forth in front of the gate between the two pastures. And he had an audience now. Angel had made a turn around, literally. She had returned to the gate and was in fact, leaning over it, in rapt adoration. I could hardly blame the old girl. Viento made a striking figure. His blue-black dappled coat glistened over the rippling of muscle, his silver mane and tail swishing in time with his step. He knew he was beautiful.

"My Viento," Lyla had said as she left the barn, "is quite a ladies' man."

"Thank goodness he's gelded," I replied.

Lyla gave a vague little smile and winked slyly. "You'll have to keep him reminded," she said.

MUSIC OF THE MOMENT

LATE SEPTEMBER AFTERNOON. Shoog blares red and yellow above the competing notes of the other hardwoods. The stridulations of tree crickets and katydids strum the air along with the rattling call of migrating bluebirds. The horses circle the apple trees on the slope of the east pasture. They have worn rings around each tree, the deepest under the centurion russet, which still gives the sweetest golden apples, though stunted and disfigured with blight. The horses don't mind imperfections. Only when I haul the barn doors open does Angel lift her head and take notice. For a brief, brimming moment I am favored with her attention, and then dropped as she swings her head back to the apples. No nicker. No acknowledgement.

The horses are in the glory of a good apple year. The old trees give as freely as they did in their prime. And it is a perfect day to be a horse, or anything. Clear and cool, with an intimate wind. The retiring sun pulls the shadows of trees and fence posts all the way into the orchard. The wedge-shaped shadow of the corner of the barn is brought there, too. Between the shadows, a golden river of light pours out of the west.

There is no contentment as deep as a horse's when the weather is fine, the pasture yields, and the worst of the flies have been knocked off by an early frost. Add apples, and tails swish to that inner music that only horses know. They need nothing from me, not even their rations of grain. It's humbling. At these times I am brought down to the reality of our bond. Without the dependency imposed upon them, the horses would not choose my company at all.

Horses live within the moment we humans are always looking beyond. This moment—dense, spiced, sweet—offers itself for the picking. Shadows halt their progression, the sun lingers on the richness of the horses' coats, playing the spectrum of follicles. In this light, even Victoria's coat shines deep rosy amber. But, for Victoria, there is little beyond this moment. While the girths of the other horses are well stocked for the winter, Victoria is sadly unprepared. The summer grasses have failed to fatten her.

Looking at Victoria brings on the specter of the coming winter. I think of the snows that sweep up the hill to the barn, sometimes so deep I can't open the doors; I think of the ice storms, the frozen buckets and frozen hose. Temperatures plunging below zero. A shadow of worry crosses my mind as I begin to mentally count the hay bales in the mow, wondering if we have gotten enough hay in to make it through the winter.

But Victoria and the other horses are as oblivious to winter coming as they are to me. They are deep in this day. Their tails swish lazily back and forth, in time with the music of the moment.

ANGEL DUST

"SHIT, SHIT SHIT!" I hiss loud enough to snap Angel out of her torpor. She flicks her ears toward the open barn door. We both watch Marilyn's progress up the slope from the house—slow, painful, yet oh-so-dogged. She stops every few steps to lean on her cane and catch her breath before moving on again. It is getting harder for her to walk from the house to the barn, but cancer has done nothing to thwart her determination. She is determined, I think to myself, clipping Angel's halter to the crossties, to drive me to insanity as her parting shot.

She still manages to make it up to the barn most mornings and afternoons when I do the chores. She positions that pink and yellow vinyl lawn chair—which I have come to despise—at the foot of the steps to the hay mow so she has a good view of the center of the barn and most of the horse stalls. From here she directs me through my chores, brandishing her cane like a riding crop. "You're using too much hay! Don't take all the shavings with the manure—shake out the fork. Why have you moved everything around? Be sure to lock up that tack room. You haven't lost the key have you? *Now,* what are you doing?"

She has arrived. A spindly silhouette in the doorway. Behind her the light is strong enough to knock her over. "I *thought* it was too early to do the chores," she exclaims, straightening her spine to pull in a long, staggering breath. "You're going for a ride." There is a lilt of delight in the last statement. She shuffles over to where her lawn chair is usually situated. I run to fetch it from the corner, where I had kicked it following her last visit.

There is little to be found in Marilyn these days. The cancer has worn her down to the bedrock of her New England stoicism. Once she has made her precarious way over the uneven planks of the barn floor to the chair, she is exhausted all over again. Finally seated, she leans back, closes her eyes, both hands gripping the handle of the cane. I sometimes make myself look at her the way she has become instead of the way I have known her. This is one of those times. Her close-cropped blond hair is a wispy surrender now, and her face is flushed and bloated with steroids. Suddenly, she opens her pale blue eyes and gives Angel a stern look of disapproval. "She's fat," she says. "You're giving her too much hay."

How many arguments have we had about this? "Angel has a wide-sprung rib cage," I reply, for perhaps the hundredth time, between clenched teeth. "It's just the way she's made." Of course she is fat, too, but I can't give Marilyn anything to work with.

"Fat," she repeats under her breath with a gleeful little grin. Marilyn likes the last word and all the words leading up to it. "Where are you going to ride?" she asks, brightening back to her old self.

"Thought I'd try McClellan's fields," I say, inspecting Angel's front hoof. Marilyn doesn't reply and I quickly realize the thoughtlessness of my response. It is a spring ritual for Marilyn and me to ride McClellan's fields. It is the first ride of the year, a chance to let the winter-bound horses "get the ginger out," as Marilyn used to say.

We'd gallop the frost-hardened fields up the long hill to the rim of pine forest. At the top, the horses would snort and stomp and catch their breath as we gazed down upon the McClellan's nest of home and outbuildings, across the road to the Rumsley's farm. It gave Marilyn pleasure to view the whole of her farm—the long, tree-lined drive that rises to the seventeenth-century farm house with Shoog, coming into bud, dominating the southeast corner. And, situated on the rise south of the house and surrounded by pastures just shrugging off snow, the barn. It always looked to me like the most enduring feature of the landscape.

"I don't think I can go with you," she says, looking down into her lap, as if riding for Marilyn was in any way a possibility. I look at her over Angel's back. It occurs to me that it was just last spring we rode McClellan's fields together. She looks up suddenly. "I may not ride until this summer." For a moment, I think maybe she will.

"Trixster will like that."

"Not if you keep over-feeding her," she snaps. "She won't be able to make it up the hill." I bury my face in Angel's neck, take a deep breath.

"What are you doing?" She asks in that tone that reduces whatever it is to an absurdity.

"I'm breathing Angel dust," I say, knowing this will annoy her. "I love the way she smells. Like summer grass and something wild."

Marilyn eyes me critically. "She smells like a horse," she grumbles. Sentimentality and all things not grounded in common sense are dismissed.

I go into the tack room for my saddle. When I come back, I am surprised to find Marilyn out of the lawn chair and leaning against Angel, her face buried in the thick fur of the horse's neck. "She does," she says, turning to me with an impish look, like she has just discovered something for the first time.

COME IN, AMANDA

THERE ARE PLENTY OF GHOSTS in this old barn, but they don't rule. The living do. They come in all forms: cats, birds, bats, spiders, horses, adults, kids, and Amanda. Most kids sweep into the barn in the spring and, like the barn swallows, are gone by September. But Amanda has been coming to the Rumsley barn for almost two years now, since she and her mother moved into Creek Side Trailer Park outside the village. They were "movers" was all Amanda had to say about how they happened to come to Galway. She didn't know how long they would stay. Maybe the school year, maybe not.

Amanda entered the barn's story the way barn cats do. It was the first warm day of early spring. Angel was on cross-ties in the center bay while I raked through her winter coat with the shedding blade. She'd been half dozing when something yanked her to attention. A small figure appeared, standing in an avenue of light between the barn doors, twisting a grass stem between her fingers. She did not enter until I motioned her in; then carefully, as if the floor might give way under her. I guessed she was about ten years old. All joints, loosely assembled, red hair pulled into a pony tail, large chestnut-colored eyes, and a dead-serious expression. Eventually, she came around to asking if she could help with the horses. "Sure," I said, "I can always use help," knowing, of course, that "helping" was code for "riding."

But Amanda did not seem eager to ride the horses, or, in fact, to get too close. It was clear that she had never encountered a horse except at a distance. She was content to watch them from the back door as they grazed or from outside their stalls at feeding time, her features compressed in frowning concentration. She would hold a grooming brush as she watched, as if it was her admission ticket should she choose to use it. I couldn't see what she was getting out of the experience, especially considering she had a four-mile ride on the clattering carcass of a bicycle to get to the barn. But she kept coming, twice a week, even in the winter when she could get a ride, just as I was bringing the horses in for their evening feeding.

"Come on in, Amanda," I'd call when I saw her standing in the doorway of the barn. Then, with quiet solemnity, she'd set to work, following my instructions exactly: cleaning and filling water tanks and buckets, rolling hay bales down from the mow, filling the cats' tins, even mucking out the run-in sheds. She quickly learned the barn's eccentricities—to watch for avalanches off the roof after a snow; to throw her weight and then some into heaving open the front doors; to stretch the water hose taut as a scream so it wouldn't freeze; to master the opening of the stall doors, each with its own terms—a push then pull, a lift then pull, a kick, a jiggle and shove; and to tease open the barn's back door so it wouldn't slide off its tracks, which happened every other week it seemed, necessitating a visit to the barn by a grumbling, tool-toting Arvis who swore all over again to fix that damn door for good and for all.

Amanda learned hungrily. I kept expecting her to ask to ride one of the horses, but she seemed content to simply watch them, muttering in a sing-song voice that sounded like the babble of an underground stream. Amanda's somber manner and shadowy home life puzzled me until I stopped thinking about it. I looked forward to seeing the small dark figure appear in the doorway.

One afternoon, before letting the horses out after their feeding, she paused in front of Trixster's stall with that same look of frowning concentration. She jiggled the stall door, gave it a slight push, and slid it open. But instead of letting Trixster out, she closed the door behind her. I stopped sweeping, leaned on the push broom, and watched as she extended her hand under Trixster's muzzle. Trixster snuffled it inquiringly, hoping for carrots, then blew a snort of disdain. Amanda didn't take it as such. She gave a hop of delight, turned to me and smiled. It was the sunlit side of her otherwise dour personality, and it made me laugh without knowing why. It didn't matter. Something had happened that said to Amanda: come in.

Amanda is not a big talker and never told me what she thought she shared with Trixster that day, but from then on she did not ask permission before entering the barn. She became the official Rumsley barn groomer—combing, currying, brushing, and hoof picking. Her fingers could locate and pluck out a tick from the thickest winter coat, and she relished combing out manes and tails matted in burs. Her deft fingers were her finest tools and her instruments of communication, as she stroked and probed, all the while issuing sing-song utterances that always seemed to me to come from someplace underneath.

PACKING IT IN

THERE'S NO GETTING AROUND IT. The long, dallying fall has finally packed it in. Yesterday was a frantic rush of wind and leaving. This morning, as Arvis informed me, the temperature plunged to twelve degrees. The stillness is resolute. Like what is left here is all that's left anywhere. We're in this together now, the horses, the cats, and I.

As I walk up to the barn, the four mares stand peering over the fence at me from the west side of the barn; Archie and Viento watch from the east side. I am the focal point of their lives now and will be for the next five months. No more taking my time getting up to the barn. I feed at regular hours in the winter, like keeping a furnace stoked so the fire won't go out. So it's early mornings now with the dawn just cracking through the horizon, salmon pink or daylily orange. It enlivens the spirit to be up early enough for the winter sunrise, but the body is otherwise inclined.

"Packing it in" aptly defines the approach of winter in the Northeast. The barn swallows that strung the barn with their endless peregrination to and from the nest have successfully raised two broods in the now-empty nest in the barn joists and flown south along with the other migratory birds. The birds that winter here have packed away their songs and chip at the silence with sharp, jabbing sounds. The wild turkeys no longer lead their broods through the pastures, but hunker deep in the hemlock forest. I haven't seen deer in the pastures since they turned from summer russet to the gray, tree-bark hue of their winter habitation. The grasses that flared green in November with a final sugar surge are spent. The cats cluster in the hay mow. The horses keep close to the barn.

And the *Argiope aurantia*, or golden orb weaver, is no longer poised at the edge of her web on the outside of the small, square window on the north side of the barn. The web was strung from the leaves of the zinnias in the window box to the top corner of the window frame. Amanda and I watched her activities all summer. A large, black spider with a yellow track pattern on her back, she was as conspicuous as a spider could be, yet no one except Amanda and I ever noticed her. Those I pointed her out to cringed in horror. But if they had spent a little time observing her, I think they might have become as charmed as Amanda and I came to be, if not for her own physical beauty then by the artistry of her web. It is a typical orb design, with threads radiating out from a hub like spokes on a wheel. What makes it her own is a little zigzag pattern woven through it which looks very much like writing. The purpose of this "signature" is not known, but has given the spider one of her other common names, the golden writing spider. She not only constructs a web of architectural genius but revises it each night, consuming the old and rebuilding it in the same place the next day. No one knows the reason for this either.

In this complicated and obsessively edited web, the spider captures whatever flies or creeps too close. Not just stable flies and mosquitoes, but grasshoppers, crickets, even wasps and the occasional dragonfly. The golden orb weaver only lives for one season, and when the weather began to turn toward fall, she abandoned her nest-revision and insect-capturing duties and dedicated herself to weaving three egg sacs, each about the size of a marble, suspended from the corners of the window frame. She stood guard over the sacs until the first hard frost claimed her. The thousands of tiny eggs she laid will winter inside the sacs, in temperatures that may dip to twenty below.

All winter I will watch the three little brown balls dangling precariously

from their fraying tether. It seems impossible that they could survive the winter. If they do, on one warm spring day, tiny replicas of the mother will be released on the air and balloon their way to start a new life. Amanda says she will come every day this spring so she won't miss the day they catch the wind on their tiny sails. She has such faith in things.

GOODBYE, VICTORIA

THE WINTER WAS A BACK BREAKER.

Temperatures dropped from the high forties to below zero in a day. Every living thing on the farm was hit hard, especially Victoria. The abrupt cold brought on a binding case of colic. That morning I discovered her thrashing about in the run-in shed; a few hours later, Dr. Schecter had put her down. All those months of treating the old mare for one ailment after another—arthritis, rain scabs, puncture wounds—and worrying over her plummeting body weight and lack of appetite came to this: an empty stall with only a name plaque to show that she had been.

Truth is, Victoria should have been put down before winter had a chance to knock her down. But keeping Victoria upright was her owner's obsession and my job. She was a problem, a case, a bafflement. Somewhere in there was a horse, too, but I'm afraid I lost sight of that.

My last memory of Victoria is the night before she came down with colic. I see her leaving the barn after the evening feeding, swaying from side to side like the lone survivor of last call. She paused in the alleyway to right herself before ambling out to the run-in shed she shared with the other mares, her towering, spindly frame lost in the heavy weather-proof blanket. She stood in the run-in shed gazing out on the snow-locked fields and expelled a long, beleaguered groan that seemed to acknowledge her vulnerability.

I still can't get used to Victoria's vacant stall, or the space where she might have been in the furthest corner of the run-in shed. It's as if the emptiness there has been reconfigured in her likeness, with all her attendant poses and vices. I still give her stall a wide berth when I walk by to avoid being bunted by her habitual head toss. I see her dozing by the south corner of the barn in the morning sun, leg cocked, listing sideways, or lurching into a gallop, legs akimbo, as she struggles to keep her balance following the other horses in from pasture.

Victoria's owner once showed me a picture of Victoria when she was a hunter/jumper in national competition. The image of the magnificent 17-hand bay in the photo is nowhere on this farm. But my enduring vision of Victoria isn't the sleek, muscled athlete she once was or the broken down old horse she came to be. It's here, in this barn, a little over two years ago.

Marilyn, her granddaughter, Lilly, and I were bringing the horses in for their evening feeding. This was before Marilyn learned of her illness, and our conversation still revolved around horses. We were discussing Victoria's long list of ailments and wondering why, even with the pasture at its summer peak, she failed to gain weight. Three-year-old Lilly was concentrating on Victoria the horse, not Victoria the problem. For reasons we could never figure out, Lilly chose the shambling old mare as her favorite among the horses. She insisted Victoria was beautiful, and loved to run her hands down the long, white blaze on her forehead. We had to watch the two closely, though, because of Victoria's habit of head tossing, which could have catapulted Lilly across the barn.

But this day we weren't watching. When we finally turned away from the subject of Victoria the problem to Victoria the horse, we froze. Victoria had inclined her head over the stall door and Lilly had wrapped her arms around it, hugging her like she would never let go. Both horse and child had their eyes closed in a state of mutual bliss. Victoria didn't move, and neither did Marilyn nor I.

Victoria's name plaque remained on the stall door until the following spring, when a new boarder arrived. It is stored in one of the trunks in the tack room with the others: Shadow Dancer, Magic, Lizzie, Serendipity, Foxy Lady, Maisy, Maya.

WINTER FROM HERE

STANLEY ORZOLECK'S BARN is a landmark in Galway. Like the Rumsley barn, it's been converted from a threshing barn to a dairy barn. It dates back to the early eighteen hundreds and is emblematic of the agrarian tradition that still defines this town. Its fieldstone understory is cut deep into the bank and once sheltered Stanley's herd of Holsteins. Even in the worst of winter, Stanley said, the heat from the cows would curdle the milk. Stanley is given to hyperbole, being one of the town's legendary storytellers.

The barn stands abandoned since multiple sclerosis forced Stanley off the farm and into the county-run nursing home. The new owners don't seem to know what to do with it, so they have done nothing. More slates blow off the roof each spring, pigeons fly into the silos through missing aluminum plates, and green paint sloughs off the siding and wafts across Lake Road. You can see through gaps in the boards of the siding now, into the barn's murky interior.

When I visit Stanley I don't mention the barn's decline. Maintaining his barn was a matter of supreme pride. Luckily, he doesn't ask about it, though I always feel he wants to. We talk about the weather instead. There's a lot to talk about there, because like all farmers, Stanley takes the weather personally.

The winter of 2011 was a meaty topic. He called it an "open winter," the worst kind for farmers. Without snow cover, cold sneaks fox-deep into the soil, freezing out bulbs and weakening roots. "Hay crop comes up late and lazy," he said, "like some offspring you can't get out of the house to earn their keep."

I didn't see him for a couple months after we had this conversation because winter hit the next day, set on making up for lost time. In fact, it brought in extra troops, specialized in inflicting all manner of misery.

By mid-January open winter was over, the cold locked in, and we were buried in three feet of snow. It came almost every day in one manifestation or the other. The Inuits have hundreds of identities for snow, but Stanley had a few of his own: the Currier and Ives snow of Christmas cards—all fluff; the Genghis Khan snow—charges in from the Northeast, immediately immobilizing everything; the Hippo snow—wet and heavy enough to collapse barn roofs, trees, and power lines. That winter brought all of these, as well as icy rain that hung off the horses' fur and manes in long icicles and formed dagger-like fangs on ledges and overhangs.

To me, the biggest threat was a barn-roof avalanche. The ice and snow that built up on the Rumsley barn's tin roof chose its own moment to slide off in spectacular falls, meeting the earth in thunderous applause. If my timing was unfortunate, I could be buried until spring. More than one barn cat has been. It's a relief to walk up to the barn and see the avalanche happened without me—relief diminished somewhat by the effort it takes to shovel through waist-high snow to get to the doors.

But by March winter had lost its bluster. Its fangs were worn down to milk teeth. I was still wary, but the horses weren't. They could always see what's coming long before I could. They went spring crazy, blowing, bucking, and chasing one another into the ice-packed fields. The barn cats launched into early heat, and a house finch broke into song off in the orchard. A rap song, more rant than rhapsody. I'll bet there was a lot in there about what a bitch of a winter it was.

I told Stanley all this the next time I visited. He allowed that there were worse things than an open winter. It was so warm in his room that day I had to take off two of my layers. He was just finishing up his lunch. "Yeah," he said, dropping his spoon into his half-eaten vanilla pudding, "there were worse winters." Then he told me of winters so cold, so cruel, he thought spring was something he'd only heard about. He recalled the famous winter of '64 and the ice storm that took out lines from "here and gone," of nine days huddled around a woodstove, of breaking ice off the pond, of milking his herd by hand. "At least the barn was warm," he chuckled. After that there was the lacuna of nothing said, when he didn't ask about the barn again.

GETTING THE HAY IN

MOST EVERYONE IN GALWAY who doesn't grow their own gets hay from the Slovak farm, a half mile south from the four corners on Parkis Mills Road. Before Marilyn's illness, Slovak's fields were one of our favorite rides. During the summer we could only ride the perimeters, but before the grass was up we could ride through the middle of the fields at full gallop, taking one after another as they undulated all the way to the Slovak's modest white farmhouse. There, Marilyn would find Slovak or his sister, Nellie, in either the barn or garden and ask the question she'd been asking for as long as I knew her: "When's the first cutting?" The answer never varied: "Second week in June."

Nature be damned, Slovak is a man who does not stray from a decision once made. Only God knows how he's gotten away with it. Harvesting hay is a chancy business and totally dependent upon prevailing weather conditions. The prime time to cut is the week or two between peak and overcooked. Once cut, there must be four straight days of good weather to tedder and dry the grass. Cut too late, it loses its nutrients; cut and rained on, it becomes mulch. Hay baled before it dries will mold; worse, it can combust and burn down your barn. Somehow, Slovak's slavish devotion to the second week in June has eluded disaster.

It is inevitable that the getting-in-of-the-hay must be done on the hottest day of the summer. At least, it has been so since I began helping unload the harvest of Slovak's fields of orchard grass, timothy, and red clover into the Rumsley barn. It is the custom of this horse-farm community that neighbors help one another during haying season, just as people did during threshing time a hundred or so years ago. That hasn't changed. What has changed is that Marilyn is gone and Slovak has had two strokes since last season. But even though he cannot speak an intelligible sentence and walks with a cane, Nellie says with a shake of her head, "I can't get the old Swede off the baler." She helps with the haying and attends him as if he were a baby bird.

So here we are again on what will be the hottest day of the summer. The production goes like this: Slovak backs the hay wagon up to the barn where the two massive doors have been hauled open as far as they will slide on their tracks. Frank Logan mops his forehead by the elevator, ready to toss on the first bales. Up in the hay mow, Arvis and Ralph McClellan brace themselves for stacking. That's the worst job. The mow is always twenty degrees hotter than the rest of the barn. There's no automatic fan to push the air around like in the Logan's new, state-of the-art barn. My job is to pitch the bales off the wagon to Nellie and Janine to haul to the elevator. Slovak, this year balancing on a cane, teeters in the shadows by the stalls, waiting for the pterodactyl elevator to throw its belt as it does every twenty bales or so. Like Slovak, the elevator has its own way of doing business. It is always Slovak who resets and tightens the belt, grunting and sweating and swearing under his breath. No one else can possibly do this. "Must be Slovak is the only one with the right wrench," Arvis mumbles.

But something is lacking this year, as vital to the process as Slovak's wrench. Something Marilyn would have certainly pointed out to us, except it is Marilyn that is missing.

In the early years, Marilyn helped stack hay in the mow with Arvis until he almost pitched her out four years ago. Since then, she focused her considerable administrative skills elsewhere. She counted hay bales, as Arvis used to say, to the blade; tested their weight and passed judgment on the quality. "You still expect to get two dollars for a bale this light, Slovak?" Or, "This year's bales are awful heavy, Slovak. Did it dry long enough?" Slovak didn't say much more then than he does now. It was a nod or a shake of the head.

She directed Nellie, Janine, and me at the wagon and Frank at the elevator, and, from a safe distance, Arvis in the mow. She insisted that each broken or suspect bale be returned. Striding about the barn with her face flushed and wearing a halo of agitated swallows, she was breathless with exertion though she never lifted a bale—not that she was opposed to hard work, but administering the production was work enough. This was her theatre. I can still see her with hay fork in hand, testing and rejecting triumphantly. Last year, she was forced to direct from the plastic lawn chair that now rests, folded, against the stairs to the hay mow. Using her cane as a sort of baton, she counted each bale that lurched up the elevator to the mow.

It's less a production this year. It's still the hottest day and we still sweat and swear. The old dinosaur continues to be revived by Slovak's magic wrench. It seems everyone knows their job and we even manage to count the bales fairly accurately. No one tests the weight or judges the quality of the hay. The broken bales are tossed in the mulch hay area. No bales are sent back.

After the stacking is done, the wagons and elevator driven away, and everyone stumbled home, I pitch loose hay into the mulch hay bay and sweep up seed heads and dust from the wide floor boards. Then I inhale the summer smell of coumarin, so ripe it lifts me off my feet. The hay dust still floats on the air, catching in spider webs and suspended in the tide of sunlight that slants through the siding and windows. The swallows have settled back on their nests attached to one of the barn's crossbeams. The little brown bat hangs from the ridgepole, far above the disturbances below. From a shadowed corner of the barn, a half-grown barn cat regards the new castles of hay. I slide the heavy doors closed and leave the cats to their kingdom.

BARN CATS

THE COUNT LOOKS DOWN ON ME from atop a hay bale. This is the year of the black cat. For a few years there was a predominance of gray tigers, then calicos, even a year when the cats were mostly Manx. The population fluctuates between five and fifteen depending on the appetite of the winter. Few live past their first summer. If winter doesn't take them, coyotes, fox, hawks, or bigger, meaner cats do.

I never know where they come from. They seem to be a conjuring of the barn, its own magic trick. One day, there's a shadow disappearing into another shadow. Some sad refugee dropped off, starved out, or chased away from wherever it was. Another shadow. Only shadows at first in a barn that harbors shadows. They could be my imagination. By spring, kittens. Not my imagination. Mewling in the hay mow, darting underneath the horses' feet, slipping between the wall boards or through the floor boards to the barn's understory, or outright abandoned in the farthest reaches of the barn by a mother who has no idea what to do with them.

Barn cats can be a fierce and alien lot. Most are born coded with a keen distrust of humans—a handy survival tool for barn cats. The Count earned his name having made it through two winters. Somewhere in the hay mow are at least four females. I don't see them until they hear the rattle of their food poured into the tin pie plates in the corner of the mulch hay bay. The neighbors say I shouldn't feed them. They consider them vermin. But one person's vermin is another person's coddled pet. I adopted a runty black kitten from the last litter—anyone's version of a hissing ball of vermin—

and now she could fit anybody's criteria for a spoiled pet. She has even assumed regal airs now that she is fed Sheba, has a fire to curl up in front of, and a cocker spaniel to intimidate.

Now that I've shared this barn's story with them, I can't shove barn cats into the catch-all vermin bin. I have discovered they are individual planets of personality. Each has its own take on the resident horses. Most stay out of their way, but others seem to have a sense of awe about them. When I see a barn cat sitting before the stall doors, gazing up at the huge beasts peering down at them, I wonder if they are adrift in the irony of their lot: who's the predator here anyway?

One little gold tabby that appeared at the barn the same year I did often comes to mind. I called her the equestrienne cat. She was devoted to Marilyn's long-retired trail horse, Serendipity.

Seren was a shipwreck. Her ribs and hip bones jutted out of her hide, and she frequently lost her balance and wobbled precariously when let out to pasture. Her back was so deeply swayed it held a pool of water after a rain, but in her stall it held a pool of golden fur. Each night, the tabby climbed up the side of the stall and alighted on Seren's back. After a little kneading and circling, she'd curl up in the deepest hollow, purring softly, exchanging comfort and warmth.

Marilyn was not sentimental about cats, horses, or anything else that I recall. She was passionate about horses, to be sure, but she was also a practical woman who had the profitability of a business to defend. When a horse was past prime it was sold or given away. A horse that was beyond use was put down. Seren's case was the exception. After lengthy monologues on why Seren should be put down before winter—while I sat mutely by, having learned that my presence, not my input, was required—Marilyn would always conclude, "but not quite yet."

The little gold tabby helped keep that difficult decision at bay, just as her perch atop Seren kept her out of the reach of predators. With Seren's decline, the cat seemed to become a part of her, and even managed to stay atop the old horse as she made her way out to pasture in the morning. Once Seren parked herself under her favorite apple tree, the tabby would hop down to go about her daily hunting, never straying too far from the horse or the apple tree. With the tabby on her back, Seren never took a misstep. As Marilyn said, the old mare was the best trail horse she ever had. She remembered her responsibility to the rider—be it cat or human.

The tabby and Seren are long gone now. But, for me, they remain a part of the landscape: the spindly old mare leaning against an apple tree, the gold tabby curled up on her back. The world and its hungers at bay.

VIENTO

HE WAS NOTHING BUT TROUBLE, but despite it or because of it, you fell in love. He wouldn't have it any other way.

Viento was an audacious rogue. With Archie as his reluctant accomplice, he amused himself by regularly upending the fifty-gallon water tank by the well house and the feeding bins in the run-in sheds and dragging them out to the middle of the pasture. He removed Archie's and his own fly masks and halters and stashed them where they have never been found. At least once a week he broke through the fencing separating the front from back fields, agitating the mares into violent heat, leaving Archie contentedly grazing on the other side, savoring, no doubt, the absence of his adventure-some pasture-mate.

Viento had no use for men—Arvis included—but loved women, whether horse or human, and could not abide rejection from either. He was twelve hundred pounds of dapple-gray brawn wrapped around a gooey heart. A sharp word would send him into a funk that would last until you paid the price for his forgiveness. "He's very sensitive," Lyla, his owner, had told me with downcast eyes as if speaking of the Pope. "He is deeply wounded by a harsh word or touch." I tended to discount Lyla's dramatizations, but I soon realized she knew her horse.

Over the years I've heard a lot of advice from horse owners about how to deal with difficult horses. Marilyn, whom I heard the most from, believed in unequivocal dominance. Horses needed to know who was in charge. Petite though she was, Marilyn was no pushover, lustily throwing her 120

50

pounds into shoving horses around, and commanding them in a voice that could singe hair. I started out by following the path of my own nature, which proved to be completely unsuccessful. Horses bullied me. Eventually, I graduated from pushover to default leader, sort of the way one becomes manager of the local convenience store. But I never came up with a "way" of dealing with horses en masse. Each horse, I discovered, was an individual case. Some responded to a firm hand, others needed nothing more than to be shown the rules and then left to follow them; some never tested you, some did nothing but. Some were affectionate, others stolidly aloft. Viento was yet another story. I could not treat him like a horse at all.

The slightest misstep or careless gesture could launch Viento into the next field. A stern directive to move forward would weld him to the ground; a tug on the halter, and he would throw up his head and snort his outrage; a tap with a riding crop would escalate his mania. He responded only to unequivocal capitulation. Once demands were traded for coaxing, the black fires in Viento's eyes tempered to embers. His ears twitched back and forth to the pitch of my voice. His head lowered, the defiance that roared from his nostrils softening to a blow of acceptance. I learned that to lead Viento required a touch that was as willing to give as to receive. Once he had taught me that, he would follow me anywhere. He most loved to be stroked and groomed. As soon as I laid the brush to his withers, he would press his cheek against my side, his eyes already half closed, fringed by long, silver-blue eyelashes.

It was easy to fall in love with Viento.

ANGEL'S DESCENT

I LOVE ANGEL. I've loved her since the first day I saw her fourteen years ago. Marilyn found her for me through her network of horse breeders—a full Arabian, of excellent breeding, and far more money than I had intended to spend. But she was too perfect to pass up—the ideal size and temperament. And she was beautiful. So beautiful! She is mostly white now, but when I bought her she had flecks of chestnut sprinkled throughout her coat. Her eyes are large, dark, soulful. Every inch of her is arched and elegant.

I have always thought she is too good for me. Angel thinks so too.

Angel still moves like a filly, dancing on air, head and tail aloft, all grace and beauty, except for the encumberment of the rider who never seems to get the dance steps right. I am a bit on the clumsy side and have finally settled on the sad truth that I am a poor hunt-seat rider. Angel has left me in the air a few times, but mostly she has recovered me, bucking my butt back into the saddle or coming to a full stop while I right myself.

Within the hierarchy of the front pasture, Angel was, at the time of Archie and Viento's arrival, queen. She had endured years of bullying from Marilyn's big brood mares, but Trixster and Victoria were malleable and Mongoose was still learning the dynamics of the herd hierarchy. Angel was first one in and out of the barn at feeding time, and she shepherded the other mares around the pasture like a hen turkey.

The arrival of Archie and Viento did nothing to unsettle Angel's status, since the mares and geldings were kept in separate pastures. But it sure unraveled her dignity. In truth, Angel disgraced herself. Viento's high stepping on the opposite side of the fence sent Angel into intense, traumatic heat. She stalked the fence line, calling to him in a skirl that raised the hair on your arms. When he cocked his head to acknowledge her, she'd swing her rump to him and flash her flaming red vulva. She could have landed a plane with the signal. The other mares stayed out of her way. They knew she was liable to do anything in her state. And she was.

Angel does not jump. Early in our relationship she made this clear. She also refused to bushwhack and didn't particularly like getting her feet muddy. So it was a real surprise to me when, after franticly running the fence line, she tried to launch herself over it.

Angel was right. She is not a jumper. As Marilyn had unfailingly pointed out to me, fine boned as Angel may be, she is of ample girth. It was this that did not clear the fence. She balanced on the top rail for an instant before it gave under her weight, dumping her into a tangle of wild grape vine, where she kicked and squealed and thrashed until she managed to free herself.

By the time Angel had regained her footing and a little composure, Viento had dismissed her. He was so beguiled by the act of prancing, lifting his legs higher with each step, that he had forgotten the purpose for it. While Angel was brought into the barn, her cuts and bruises treated, Viento pranced on, back and forth, in love with his own free-floating gait and spectacular beauty.

Archie, who had been sedulously engaged in grazing throughout, lifted his head once, snorted, and went back to business.

THE GIRL, THE CUTTER, THE PACER

"A MARE IN HEAT could spark this place up." Boo Womack stood gazing around the barn, slapping his rasp against his leather chaps. I try to ignore the farrier's grim pronouncements as much as possible, so I fetched the first horse to be trimmed. It was so cold Viento's breath stood on the air like it was sculpted in stone. Boo Womack always brought the worst weather with him.

As obstreperous as Marilyn was, she did not curse—something to do with her austere New England upbringing—except when it came to Boo Womack, who she only referred to as "that miserable old son of a bitch." "Horses need trimming." Sigh. "Time to call that miserable old son of a bitch," or "That miserable old son of a bitch charged me ten dollars extra to do the foal." Boo was not really old. It was his permanent stoop and shut-tered gaze that made him seem so. But miserable he surely was.

A farrier's work is old-world hard. There's plenty of new science on cor-rective trimming and shoeing, but the tools for trimming a horse's hooves have changed little in a hundred years: hoof knife, rasp, clippers, and one hell of a strong back. It's hours of back-bending work, supporting a horse's hoof on your knee or between your legs, sometimes as the horse is leaning on you, pulling away, cow-kicking, or attempting to run you over. It is no wonder that Boo's nature aligned with the slope of his spine.

After Marilyn passed away and I assumed all barn chores, I would assist Boo during trim days, standing at the horse's head while he walked around his subject like a trial attorney assessing the intimidation threshold of a wit-ness, slapping his rasp against his chaps and scowling as he appraised stance and posture, balance and flare. Then, with a prodigious throat clearing, he'd bend to work, his canvas butt all that was visible to me, as he dispensed his world view amid grunts, profanities, and the snap of clippers.

"Rack of bones," he used to say of Victoria as he lifted her hind foot, almost toppling her over. "You gonna put her down or just let her crash?" Trixster was pigeon-toed, Angel hay-bellied, and of Archie: "Thoroughbred?" he snorted. "Looks more like a mule got cozy with a moose."

His view of most farriers: hacks who didn't know a rasp from a nail file; of most horse owners: shouldn't keep chickens, let alone horses; and for the rest of humanity: a wad of sputum.

He did not suffer supercilious horses. He put an end to Viento's antics with a quick knee to the gut, without pausing in his diatribe about the staggering stupidity of his last customer.

He was a miserable son of a bitch, all right, but a good farrier—and interspersed with invectives on all things human, animal, and otherwise were garnets of wisdom. From his travels to horse farms throughout Upstate New York, he gathered prime tidbits—who was looking to board, sell, or unload horses, who had the best price on hay, what feed mix added weight to hard keepers, and who might be going in or out of business. He could tell the medical history and soundness of a horse simply by looking at its coronary band and the set of its hooves. He knew almost as much as Dr. Schecter about treating lameness, arthritis, puncture wounds, and inflammations. And if he never had a good thing to say, his silence was golden.

Since the knee in the gut adjustment, Viento was all acquiescence, at least during trimmings. I had something to learn from the miserable old son of a bitch, I thought to myself. The horse stood with the manners of a choir boy while Boo's gaze climbed from his hooves to the interior of the barn. I expected another comment on an impending conflagration, but his eyes settled on the cutter, sooted in dust and spider webs in the east bay. Perhaps a scolding about cluttering a barn with useless relics? Or maybe a lecture on the mistreatment of antiques?

"Had one just like this," he said, nodding toward the cutter. "An 1877 Albany. Come 'crost it in the back of a barn being took down." He laid a palm on Viento's shoulder. The horse lifted his front foot like a circus performer. "Took me a year to restore it." He bent to his trimming. "Put new upholstery to it, welded the runners, rebuilt the shaft." He let down Viento's hoof, slid his hand along the horse's girth and flank and down his left rear leg. The foot lifted in accommodation. "Painted it blue."

There was rasping and grunting and heavy breathing. "I bought an old pacer to pull it. She was a real high stepper. Loved to show off." He stood, his face squeezed tight as he tried to stretch out his back. After a long pause, he said, "Caught a girl with it." And left it there, to call to mind all kinds of disturbing images. "Most of 'em," he continued at last, "wouldn't go with a boy didn't have a truck. But this girl," he shook his head in wistful wonder, "she loved that cutter. And," he added with a wink that contorted his face, "that buffalo blanket."

He slapped Viento on the rear, a sharp that's-that to the job and the reminiscing. I wanted to ask him what happened with the girl, the cutter, and the pacer, but I decided to leave it at that. The miserable old son of a bitch did not like to be bothered when tallying up the bill.

WIND SPIRIT, EARTH SPIRIT

THIS SUMMER, the tranquility of the farm is interrupted every Saturday afternoon at three. No transcendent moments of field gazing, bird watching, or working in the garden. My attention is focused on two ten-year-old girls who come for riding lessons. Regina is the teacher. I call her the sorcerer. No one has such magic with kids and horses. I assist the sorcerer, mostly by staying out of the way. The riders are Tina and Amanda. Once Tina's mother drops them off at the driveway, they race one another up to the barn, chattering the entire way, like two birds just flown in from another hemisphere.

Amanda—shy, withdrawn, taciturn—has recently broken out of herself. Since she and Tina discovered their mutual love for horses, they have become almost inseparable, and Amanda has been driven to match Tina's horsemanship. Now the two take riding lessons together and Tina's mother does the chauffeuring, which works out well now that Amanda's bicycle seems to have finally been put to rest. The side effect of this new friendship, however, is that Amanda has adopted the flighty persona of her friend, at least when they are together. I hardly know her then. Even without Tina, Amanda carries traces of her affect, talking more than usual in a sing-songy voice, trailing the last syllable off in space.

Since she no longer has a bicycle, the Saturday riding lesson is the only time I am sure to see Amanda at the barn these days. Occasionally, she'll beg a ride from her mother or one of her mother's friends, who drop her off at the bottom of the drive before speeding off, much the way I have seen people rid themselves of stray cats. I often find myself looking down the drive for her, hoping to see that small figure half running, half lurching up the driveway. It surprises me how much her presence has moved into this barn.

As the girls race up to the barn, they are all shrieks and flutter, with much urgent news to share despite having spent all week in school together. Thankfully, they become hushed and reverent once they enter the barn. Horses are what they worship, and the barn is the place of horses. The lesson begins with grooming and tacking up. Tina is eager to get out into the riding ring, but for Amanda, grooming is the best part. She can't help taking her usual care with mane and tail, leaning into the horse, finding her internal, underground voice. Tina and Trixster have already done three laps around the ring before Amanda is mounted.

Angel and Trixster have settled into this weekly obligation. Trixster is a warrior and will do what is asked of her, but Angel is less obliging. She should not be asked to serve as a lesson horse, she protests, blowing and pawing the ground. If she could roll her eyes, she would. But this is all for show. Her only real display of resistance is to ignore Amanda's command to move forward until she absolutely has to obey.

Horses take on a sacrificial attitude when Amanda leads them out to the riding ring. She cannot weigh more than seventy-five pounds, but once she's in the saddle, Angel visibly sags, looking more like a pack animal preparing for a trek up the Himalayas than a riding horse. But under Tina they soar. Heads swing up, ears prick forward. They fairly prance around the riding ring. Tina does not seem to be riding as much as soaring. While Tina does figure eights at a canter, Amanda plods steadily on, looking like a marionette with the strings cut. She is not a natural rider.

You would think this might breed bad feelings between the two girls. Nothing can make a kid feel worse than to be bested at what they love. But no one is bested. Regina, who understands kids like she understands horses, does not heap praise on either girl. She doesn't seem to give many commands, either, but somehow the message is understood. Regina says each girl has a share of the horse spirit. Tina's is the wind spirit, and Amanda's the earth spirit. Tina loves the wind in her face; Amanda loves the horse itself. While Tina is impatient after riding to get on to the next thing, Amanda sinks into her natural rhythm of grooming, probing for ticks, bruises, or knots. After the riding lesson, Tina chases cats in the hay mow. Amanda hand-grazes one of the horses out front of the barn where the grass is especially lush.

By the end of the lesson, the girls come back together, re-assembled into a flighty, slightly manic twosome that forgets to close the barn doors behind them as they race one another down the hill, chattering like wrens, circling one another, then tumbling in the grass, once, twice, before finally being taken into the car.

SARAH AND GARTH

ON MY WAY TO THE RUMSLEY BARN on a mid-July morning, I pedal past the Logan farm on the right, just uphill from the four corners, where Parkis Mills Road intersects Hermance. Janine Logan is putting her Arab, Breeze, through her paces, preparing for another endurance ride. At the north corner, Sarah Wylie pops up amid billows of hydrangeas, squints into the sun and waves her trowel at me. On the south corner, the Genoveses' seldom-ridden but greatly pampered quarter horses chase one another along the fence line to get a better look as I pass, as if I am something new. I take a left, and I'm at the Rumsley barn in about three minutes.

Having all these horse farms so close together makes us a tight little community. We ride together from time to time and share horse chores when one or the other is away. We share other things, too—what we have too much of in our gardens, or seeds, plants, gossip, berries, knowledge, troubles.

Knowledge is what I need most, and I have borrowed a great deal of it from the other women who, except for Lisa Genovese, have worked with horses all their lives. From them I have learned how to identify and treat the surprising multiformity of ailments that can befall an animal as strong as a horse, and we have all beat on the same drum of how to get horses to do what you want them to do. Sarah also knows every horse trail in Galway, those that are there and those that are there only for Sarah. Without Sarah, you'd never find them.

Sarah and her husband, Harvey, farm ninety of the fattest acres in Galway. They grow hay for their horses, raise two beef cattle and one milk cow.

Sarah's garden pumps out every vegetable in the catalog. The Wylies grow raspberries, blueberries, and their orchard of Northern Spies gives fruit every year. Chickens free-range through the orchard and barnyard, their numbers rising and falling in tune with the fox and fisher population. Somebody's kids are always staying at the Wiley house, mixed in with the chickens and cats and other critters. Sarah seems to be everybody's caretaker. But when she's on her horse, Garth, she's something else. A little scary.

Garth is a handsome black Morgan who spends most of his days dozing in the sun, one leg cocked, head down, eyes closed. The picture of contentment and docility. But under saddle he steps out of Garth and becomes more of a Zephyr or Tornado. Once the girth is tightened, Garth begins to churn, snorting like a steam engine, his muscles bunched and ready to detonate. Sarah, barely one hundred pounds, mounts this broiling beast as if she caught a thermal onto his back.

Riding with Sarah can be terrifying, especially in the spring, when all horses go a little crazy. Even Marilyn wouldn't do it. I did. Once. I have not forgotten the experience, nor has Angel, I'm sure.

It all began tamely enough. We met at the four corners, Sarah and I exchanging greetings while Garth tossed his head in impatience and Angel looked archly on. We rode up Parkis Mills Road for half a mile, Garth setting the pace with a nice swinging trot. I was lulled into the rhythm of the ride as I gazed between the twin peaks of Angel's ears at the jostling of Sarah's black pony tail and Garth's black tail. Then, a quick turn up to the Slovak's fields. The twin black flames diminishing, lost at the tree line, like a rabbit down a hole.

There was no holding Angel back. Spring crazy and in the first hard heat of the season, she was not going to let Garth out of her sight. Into the rabbit hole we followed, down a rutted trail crisscrossed by ropes of exposed roots and fallen logs. The trail snaked back and forth upon itself, growing more treacherous as we rode. Angel struggled to keep her footing, managed to jump a log, cross a stream. I hung on with everything I had, not sure if that was enough, not able to see Garth or Sarah or the trail or any end to the nightmare. We were riding through hemlock forest so deep and dark it seemed we could not still be in Galway. What forest was this? Where were we going? Would it end?

As we pounded across the Gloweegie for what seemed the fourth time, a tree branch smacked against my helmet, sending me sliding over Angel's shoulder, close to falling and sure I would, until she bucked me back in the saddle. Then, off again, up the embankment and onto a trail Angel seemed to follow by Braille. I clung to her tight as a leech, head buried in mane, leaving it all up to her.

Finally, the blessing of light ahead, breaking through the hold of hemlocks. Rush of sunlight. A field as magical as Narnia. John Mechanick's east field, I realized with relief, not far from the four corners. How we arrived there while seemingly going in the opposite direction was a puzzle. But there were Sarah and Garth perfectly framed on the golden dome of the field, Garth twirling in place like a Lipizzaner, Sarah waving back at me. They were a magnificent sight, I thought later. Much later.

After that spring ride, I admired the duo of Sarah and Garth from a distance. I would catch a glimpse of them on my way to the Rumsley barn, streaking across a field, dashing up a hillside or disappearing down another rabbit hole.

One evening I remember especially well. It was deep into June, after the first cutting of hay. Sarah, after a long day loading hay into the barn, had tucked children and chickens away, and was setting out for a ride. It must have been an impulse because she was riding bareback with only a rope hackamore to contain the uncontainable Garth. They trotted across the hayfield, flushing crows scavenging the freshly shorn earth, toward the woods that separated the Wiley farm from the Slovaks'. As the day shimmered to a close behind them, they slipped from horse and rider to apparition. Darkness gathering them in, slowly at first, then into the gallop, and gone.

THE GALLOPING FIELD

THIS AFTERNOON the horses are not to be found. The pasture looks incomplete. This land, shaped by generations of ungulates, needs them as a hand needs something to hold. Their absence, poked through by bird song, sends a little prickle of panic up my spine. I hurtle my three-part whistle in the direction of the back fields. No answering whinny. But it's July, I remind myself. The horses can range far.

The horses must be in one of the adjoining fields to the west. It is easy to forget these two back fields belong to the farm. They are islands of Little Bluestem, an escaped grass of the Grain Plains, separated from the larger pastures by a phalanx of eighty-foot white pines and an impenetrable understory. I cross the back field and follow a trail of fresh manure leading to the right side of the stone wall that separates the two lower fields. Bobolinks flare out above the tops of the unmown grass, dribbling their songs behind them. I keep to the edges of the field to avoid the nests and follow the curve of the stone wall until I can see the entire length of the field to the dark rim of hemlock.

Three deer startle at the edge of the grass. They raise their tails and bunch their hind quarters for flight. Except for the slight tail twitching, they are motionless, held on the instant before leaping, heads, necks and ears branching against the backdrop of forest. As soon as I move, deer become forest, the white flash of tails all I can make of them. The grasses sough. The Bobolinks settle back into their nests. There are no horses here.

I climb the stone wall and enter the adjoining field. Once I free myself

64

from the clutches of multiflora rose, honeysuckle, and bramble, I survey the breadth of the grassland that at this hour is bisected by shadow. The horses are there, at the border between sun and shadow. They watch me with the pointedness of deer. They are wild, too. A horse among horses is always wild. They regard me as if from a distance greater than the length of the field. I walk toward them, dissolving distance. They blow a furious resignation and drop their heads to graze again.

Marilyn called this the galloping field. It is the only level land on the farm. It was perfect, she said, for conditioning horses for cross-country trials. Her daughter, Nancy, used to gallop her mare, Maisy, here. For hours sometimes. It was her contrary nature, Marilyn claimed, more than dedication to conditioning, that drew Nancy to this back field, endlessly galloping its perimeter.

She was sixteen. She didn't want to be found by anyone. I think of her whenever I cross the galloping field. The light leaves these lower fields first, the shadow of the bordering pines and hemlocks stretching across them like a black tide flooding this shimmering island of grass. I see the girl leaning into the shoulder of the horse, fearlessly galloping through the ripe summer light, plunging into darkness, then out again, the inevitable night closing in.

I have almost reached the horses now. They lift their heads and regard me. They are balanced between wildness and routine. Even my Angel could bolt. Her head is held high, eyes slanting down on me. When I rest my palm upon her neck, I know she is my horse again. She lowers her head and follows me, the others close behind. The slow rocking of their bodies is as labored as if they carried a dispiriting burden. Their burden is to follow. The routine is our common language.

ISABELLA

FOR YEARS, THERE'D BEEN TALK of a pinto pony seen passing through someone's pasture or glimpsed disappearing into the woods. The sightings were spaced so far apart it was dismissed as local folklore, until folklore became Isabella, belly high in timothy in the middle of the Slovak's prime hayfield.

The Slovaks weren't sure what she was at first. They guessed a donkey or mule until the creature beckoned to them in a sweet, high-pitched nicker. The pony let Nellie Slovak walk up to her and slip a rope around her neck, and then followed docilely as she was led into the Slovak's barn. From there, the Slovaks didn't know what to do with her. There was no telling how old she was. She was rib sprung and shaggy as a wooly mammoth with hooves that had grown so long they curled up at the toes like elf shoes. But it was clear she had been somebody's pony at one time and seemed willing to give up her wild ways to be that again.

The Brautigans, whose farm was kitty-corner to the Slovaks, came up to have a look at this curiosity. The family owned two matching Haflingers that paraded around like exhibitionists at fairs and shows, pulling a custom-designed cart. The Brautigans had no interest in adopting the wayward, wormy pony whose species, let alone breeding, was suspect. But the Brautigan children did. Three-year-old Dana and five-year-old Diesa flew to the pony as if she was just what they had been expecting. Isabella closed her eyes and buried her muzzle between the two children as they wrapped their arms around her sizeable head like they would never let go. Before their parents could form a solid protest, the pony had a name. And that was that.

Even groomed, trimmed, fattened, and de-wormed, Isabella had a permanently underprivileged look, but to the Brautigans, the pony soon outshone the fancy, honey-colored Haflingers. "Isabella raised the kids," Margaret Brautigan used to say.

Isabella taught Dana and Diesa how to ride, and a whole lot more. She would stand patiently while the kids clambered and lunged their way onto her back, but she would not take a step forward until they learned to give her the proper cues. If they yanked at her halter or raised their voices, she would shut her eyes and lock down like a safe. If they kicked her sides, she would shake violently until they slid off. She would tolerate almost anything except disrespect. She was their circus pony, then Lion King, then Dumbo, and even a princess once. She would acquiesce to almost any costume—false ears and floppy hats or ribbons, ruffles and feathers. She learned to count, nod "yes" or shake her head "no," and to bow after each performance. There seemed no end to the roles Isabella could play. The kids read to her, sang to her, composed stories for her.

And eventually outgrew her.

Isabella's role diminished as Dana and Diesa grew older, except to serve as audience to the occasional outpouring of adolescent despair. When the kids entered high school, the Brautigans moved and were forced to find another home for Isabella. She had to be very old by then, but the Logans agreed to take her in as company for one of their own retired horses that was left behind during the competitive riding season. It was a perfect rest home for Isabella—plenty of pasture, her own stall, excellent care. But Isabella did not wish to rest.

If Janine Logan happened to leave the barn door open while letting the horses in or out from pasture, Isabella took the opportunity to make her escape. Once out of the barn, she set off at a wobbly trot down the hill toward her former home with a determination that could not be called back. She would charge into the front yard and whinny at the door until the new owners, the Genoveses, answered the call and led her into her old barn. Then the Logans would come and fetch her. This became routine. Isabella never forgot the family her heart belonged to.

Horses are creatures of habit, but Isabella was her own creature. The last time she escaped, she did not head down hill to the Genovese farm as she had done with each escape since the Brautigans moved away. She could not be found anywhere. The roundup crew of neighbors so experienced in searching out escaped horses, cows, and pigs could find no trace of the missing pony.

We never knew what became of Isabella, but folks in Galway still ask about her. Whenever I cross the Slovak's fields, I look for the flop-eared pinto grazing happily on timothy and alfalfa. Wishful thinking, I know.

BUTCH AND WALLY'S USED LADDER WORLD

I WAS DELIGHTED when Arvis finally agreed to replace the rusted tin roof of the back run-in shed until he told me whom he had hired for the job—Butch and Wally of the former Tom & Sons construction business. Old Tom, with sons Butch and Wally in tow, had replaced the main barn roof six years before, and I was having no success convincing Arvis that Tom & Sons without Tom consisted of two middle-aged nitwits who drank and fought a lot. But Arvis is a man who returns to the same waterhole until he dies of thirst.

"Arvis, you know old Tom is dead."

"The business isn't. His boys run it. Tom *and* Sons."

"But it's not a construction business. It doesn't even have the same name. They sell ladders."

Arvis looked at me like I had just suggested that the sun forgot to rise. "Tom and Sons has always been there." His final words on the subject.

Tom & Sons had been Tom & Sons since old Tom's grandfather started the business in 1924. It was a small, family-run enterprise specializing in the building and repair of outbuildings, with the elder Tom being the owner and his two sons his only employees. The family tradition was broken when old Tom's first son, Tom, decided to call himself Butch, and Wally was, well, Wally, and neither was likely to be the progenitor of future Toms. Butch and Wally were, in the kindest term, somewhat peculiar.

On old Tom's passing, it became evident to Butch and Wally, to whom little ever was, that they should perhaps have paid more attention to the old man's craft. Instead, they had been content to be "fetchers," hauling tools and materials up and down ladders, or holding ladders in place, or running for paint or plywood or beer.

Butch and Wally had inherited none of the previous Tom's business acumen, integrity, sense of responsibility or, for that matter, desire to work. Being fetchers was work enough. The thought of putting hammer to nail and the rest of it did not sit well with the brothers.

So Butch got an idea. He did, occasionally, when driven to it. What emerged was more accident than idea. After surveying his father's shop, Butch found—among the plethora of antique tools neither he nor his brother had any idea how to use—ladders. Many, many ladders. Extension ladders, step ladders, platform ladders, roof ladders, all in various sizes. Butch and Wally had no use for ladders, having been forced to climb them all those years. But Butch's new idea did not require them to climb ladders. They would lease ladders for jobs other people would do themselves. Thus was born Butch and Wally's Used Ladder World.

They devoted three days to painting a large sign in white paint on the back of a sheet of plywood. They placed it in front of the Tom & Sons sign which had graced the front of the shop for ninety years. Several of the more impressive ladders were displayed against the front of the shop, the extent of the heavy lifting Butch and Wally planned to do from that point forward. To convey their earnest entrepreneurial spirit and good will, they stationed themselves, with a case of beer between them, on either side of the sign to await their first customers, apparently having no idea that two besotted men leering from either side of Butch and Wally's Used Ladder World, might send a contrary message. In fact, it did, and soon Butch and Wally were forced to consider other means of support.

With no new ideas forthcoming and against all they held dear, Butch and Wally were dragged back into the construction business by force of Tom & Sons' long-standing reputation. No one seemed to have interest in leasing used ladders, but there were many who could use the services that Tom & Sons had provided all those years. So, Butch and Wally, running low on beer money, blundered along on their father's good name for a few months until the lack of old Tom on the job could no longer be overlooked. Business staggered to a fitful end. Butch was on the cusp of another idea when Arvis called. For Butch and Wally, this set off dim memories of unpleasant episodes.

When old Tom replaced the barn roof, Marilyn was very much alive and strong enough to take on the idiocy of his two sons. No beer drinking, hammer throwing, fist fights, littering of nails. No profanity. As this just about summed up Butch and Wally's repertoire, they were not likely to repeat the experience, except that now they were somewhat desperate, Marilyn was gone, and Arvis and I were less likely to get in their way.

Butch and Wally seemed pleased with themselves when their pickup bumped up to the barn the next morning with a massive extension ladder bouncing around in the back, along with old Tom's vintage wooden tool box and a case of beer. But as they were setting up their ladder against the run-in shed, another dim memory came into focus for Wally.

"You going to put those horses somewhere else?" Wally was terrified of horses. He had a nasty incident during the last job when, denied beer and fighting, he decided to make friendly with one of the foals, to which its mother made immediate and violent objection. Wally showed me the scar on his hand lest I had forgotten the incident.

"They won't bother you," I said. "There are just two old geldings in this pasture. They want no more to do with you than you do with them."

Wally squinted his eyes in grave suspicion at the two silhouettes in the distance, grazing near the south hedgerow.

"Just two old geldings," I repeated. "See you later."

Butch and Wally were not there later. Arvis was, and not in good humor. He was pushing a wheelbarrow in from the back pasture.

"Must be the weathered look," I observed. "Looks like the same rusty roof to me."

Arvis was not amused. As he thrust the wheelbarrow closer, I saw bright silver cans bouncing around inside it. "They're not like old Tom," he said, giving me an accusatory look.

"I told you."

"You got to tell me so I can hear it," he shouted, thinking, no doubt, of how he and Marilyn communicated all those years. "Fools lit out of here like they saw a ghost."

"Must have been some ghost to separate them from their beer."

"It was a horse," Arvis spit, "that damn big, gray horse."

Viento, of course, would not remain a benign figure at the far end of the pasture for long. Activity, particularly of the human kind, was sure to attract him. And then there was the ladder invitingly leaning against the run-in shed, the two men jumping up and down on the roof, and the bonus—a box of shiny objects at the base of the ladder. It all added up to an afternoon of high entertainment for Viento.

"By the time I got up here," Arvis said, "those two had an ass full of splinters from shimmying down the post and were fighting over which one of them was going to fetch their beer back from that horse."

Arvis shook his head and let go of the handles of the wheelbarrow. A few beer cans jumped out and hit the ground. He picked one up, eyed it for an instant, and popped it open. "And there you have it!"

Butch and Wally never came back for their ladder. It is now one of the barn's relics. I hear the two have started a new business—selling antiques out of their father's shop, where most everything is antique. They still call the business Butch and Wally's Used Ladder World, though. They'd put so much work into that sign.

PETER TWITCH

ABANDONED KITTENS are among the many ghosts this old barn shelters. Often I have heard the tiny mewings of the left behind like desperate prayers, and despite my best efforts, many have gone unanswered. But once Amanda entered the barn's life story, nary a kitten escaped unsaved. Even those that didn't need it. These would be quickly reclaimed by their mothers from the nesting box Amanda had carefully prepared for them in the mulch hay bay.

When Amanda caught the drift of a tiny mew, she would stiffen like a bird dog on the point, drop bucket, manure fork, or curry comb, and peer off in the direction of the hay mow with an expression of ecclesiastic rapture. Then she was off, following her ears and instinct, folding her collapsible body between hay bales and into the netherworld of the barn's recesses. After a few minutes or sometimes hours, she would surface, her red hair netted with spider webs and the detritus of a century, clutching a brood of squealing kittens in her arms or cradled in her shirt.

Peter Twitch's story was different. He didn't need finding.

Amanda and I stood staring into the stall at the gray tiger, no bigger than my fist, huddled against Mongoose's left hoof. Amanda had spotted the kitten first and would have flown to its rescue if I hadn't caught hold of her shirttail. Mongoose had not been mellowed by impending motherhood. In fact, since her owner, Jaycee, had insisted she be kept in her stall for a few days, the horse was a storm about to break. She paced, stomped, kicked the sides of her stall, and threatened anyone who came near. But at the moment, the mare was standing eerily still. Only her ears flicked back and forth as she awaited our next move.

The tiny tiger looked unperturbed. There was nothing exceptional about this kitten except that he was where he was and yet untrampled, and had an unusually long tail, which stood straight up and twitched like a current was running through it.

"I guess I'll just go in there and get that kitten," my voice bolted out of me, staggered away. Mongoose caught my intent. She flattened her ears and gave me the moon eye. The moon eye—little crescent of white that arcs above the iris when a horse is scared or very, very angry — is seldom a good sign. Amanda and I held our breath and hoped for some solution to arrive.

The water pump clicked on, clicked off. I'd forgotten to turn the water off after filling the tanks. "Amanda," I warned, holding up a forefinger and giving her my own version of moon eye.

"I won't," she assured me.

Amanda, who had finally grown confident enough to enter the barn without asking permission, who followed instructions unerringly, who did as she was told, did not this time. Before I could switch off the pump, I heard the telling creak-thunk of Mongoose's stall door being lifted, and then slid open.

I rushed back on tip toe, and let out a long-held breath as I peeked inside the stall.

Amanda stood beside Mongoose, cradling the kitten in her arms. The volatile Mongoose nuzzled the kitten experimentally, then decided it really wasn't her problem, and swung around to snatch some hay.

Amanda looked at me apologetically. "I know, I know," she mouthed as she slipped out of the stall, re-latching the door with one hand, holding the kitten against her chest with the other. I waved away the explanation she was constructing. I knew.

Kittens, by virtue of being kittens, are cute, but Peter Twitch tested that principle to the limit. Though I never let on to Amanda, who loved him unrelentingly, this kitten was, as I failed to gather at first glance, exceptional. It was hardly a wonder his mother had abandoned him. He was the homeliest kitten I had ever set eyes on. Besides being a runt, with spiky fur and Marty Feldman eyes, he had a curiously long and electrified tail. But these peculiarities only served to distinguish him over his long life and tenure as the barn's self appointed concierge. It was Peter Twitch's responsibility to attend the horses each morning and evening as they entered and exited the barn. As barn greeter, he would stroll magisterially down the slope to meet whoever was arriving, and escort them up to the barn.

Peter Twitch never grew to be a handsome cat, or even a presentable cat, but he possessed a courtly manner that served him well. No matter how early or late I came up to the barn, Peter Twitch would come out to greet me—head held high and his tail, which grew even longer as he grew older, twitching with delight.

ROUNDUPS

THE "ANNUAL SPRING BREAK," we call it around here.

While the fields are winter locked, horses hunker around the barn and run-in sheds wrangling over piles of hay and waiting for the spring grass to come in. When it does, you'd think they'd be content with the beckoning green pastures opening up to them. But that's just when they get the urge to leave it all behind. See the world. After the winter snows and blow-downs, there is always at least one breach in the fence line, and once through it, the horses are off and galloping down to the four corners, farting and snorting their liberation. Then they migrate over to the Wileys' or the Genoveses' to stir up the resident horses, flaunting their freedom and squealing all kinds of inflammatory propaganda to their fenced-in brethren. Within an hour the adventure is over, the escapees led home. Shaking a can of grain is usually all it takes to bring them in from the wild.

Trixster was the only horse on the Rumsley farm with the initiative to engineer a breakout. These usually followed a six-week stint at a kid's summer camp, where Marilyn had sent her while she and Arvis were in Maine. At camp, Trixster was ridden every day by a variety of young riders whose zeal far exceeded their horsemanship. By the time Trixster was trailered back to the Rumsley farm in late August, she was hell bent.

One day back and Trixster would maneuver the bottom rail out of its post slot and scoot under it into the Horigans' cornfield, there to dine on corn until the sun came up, while her less ingenious pasture mates whin-nied beseechingly over the fence at her.

But these spring breaks and Trixster's late-August foray did not involve the entire neighborhood, the news media, or the intervention of Cowboy Jim, as the escape of the Wileys' steers did a few years ago.

Each spring the Wileys bought two young steers from a factory farm to be fattened on their own farm for slaughter in the fall. Once the steers were settled into the Wileys' alfalfa fields they grew fat and complacent, but the transition from trailer to field was the critical juncture in that attitude adjustment. Two years ago, the steers escaped by charging an unlatched gate as soon as they were unloaded from the trailer.

Usually the neighborhood roundups involve horses or an occasional pig, but steers are another matter. Nothing like the lazy, cud-chewing creatures they would become, these two were terrified and desperate for their freedom, which they managed to hold onto for a good share of the summer.

The Wileys, accompanied by a pack of neighborhood zealots, answered numerous calls of sightings only to find the steers had vanished like fog once they arrived, leaving only tracks and trampled foliage. No one could figure out how two young steers, that had known nothing but the inside of a pen crowded in with other doomed creatures, could outmaneuver a posse of town folk. Tempers flared, patience frayed, helpers drifted away. Then Cowboy Jim was called in.

Not *called in* exactly. He just showed up at the Wileys', trailer in tow, about two weeks into the hunt. He described himself as a roundup "closer." Cowboy Jim had a lot to say about himself, in fact. Apparently, he was famous.

As I turned onto Parkis Mills Road that morning on my way to the Rumsley barn, I spied the Wileys in earnest conversation with a man who looked exactly like Sam Elliot. I had to stop and investigate.

He was a cowboy, all right, from the tilted-back cowboy hat to the oversized belt buckle to the long pointy toes of his boots. Denim and leather and an Oklahoma drawl. Then he backed his showy palomino out of the trailer, fully tacked up with the largest western saddle I'd ever seen, elaborately tooled, tasseled, and edged in silver. The palomino was a lot edgier than most working horses, and I figured he'd tire himself out with all his prancing and head tossing theatrics before Cowboy Jim even hoisted himself and all that leather into the saddle.

Glen and Sarah Wiley are the most down-to-earth people I know, but I think Cowboy Jim dazzled them with his drawling promise to track, rope, and bring in their steers. I was convinced, too, and would have done anything to tag along for the roundup, but I had horses to feed and another potential boarder I hoped might actually show up this time. Turns out, I didn't miss a detail. It was headline news for almost a week.

Much to the Wileys' chagrin, Cowboy Jim was quite the self-promoter and had contacted the Daily Gazette, the Saratogian, the Albany Times Union, and various local weeklies as well as radio and TV stations, announcing his latest gig: "Cowboy to the Rescue of Local Farmer." Cowboy Jim must have written that headline himself.

The Wileys were portrayed as hapless newcomers to the farming scene, desperate for Cowboy Jim's help to recover their errant steers. People came from three towns over to stand in front of the pasture where the two steers would be if the Wileys had only been competent enough to keep them there.

For weeks, an entourage of the curious trailed Cowboy Jim on foot, horseback, and four-wheelers into the ample fields and forests surrounding Galway. The unofficial posse succeeded in driving the steers deeper into hiding and protracting the search into late summer.

Most of the followers as well as the interest of the media had begun to dwindle by the time John Mechanick called the Wileys to report that their two steers were grazing in his apple orchard. Now, John Mechanick, being an old farmer, would have coaxed those two exhausted steers into his barn with a rattle of corn in a coffee can if it hadn't been for the almost immediate and operatic arrival of Cowboy Jim and his flamboyant palomino.

With Cowboy Jim in spectacular pursuit, the steers bolted from the Mechanick property and headed down Hermance Road toward Route 147, which they all crossed, miraculously, without incident. The chase proceeded through the middle of town and into Ludlow Swamp where, I hear, Cowboy Jim actually got his rope around one of the steers. After that, things didn't go the way they were so colorfully portrayed in Cowboy Jim's media kit. Instead of the steer being pulled up short, the way the cowboy's script read, the scrawny beast yanked Cowboy Jim off his horse and through Ludlow Swamp for half a mile or so before Cowboy Jim remembered to let go of the rope. So now the steers were running lose in the impenetrable three-hundred-acre Ludlow Swamp, and Cowboy Jim had lost his belt buckle and a good deal of his swagger.

Turns out a turkey hunter found the steers at the edge of the swamp a few days later. One was snagged by Cowboy Jim's rope on a downed tree branch; the other stood forlornly nearby. They were both emaciated and past fight. The hunter untangled the rope and led the steer back to the Wileys'. The other followed dog-like behind.

The real closer didn't get the headlines that Cowboy Jim did, but he probably wasn't looking for them either.

THE McHENRY FARM

THE McHENRY FARM is the last farm before the town line, and it looks like it should have passed the way of the other family-run dairy farms that once defined Galway. Many of the small dairy farms are gone or conflated into megafarms with eight hundred cows that spend most of their days in stanchions inside cavernous steel structures, plugged into milking machines. But Freddy McHenry's stock roam his rocky pasture amid the decompositions of various junked vehicles, searching for the little grass that manages to grow between. At sunset they wind their way back into the tottering old barn where, if you happen past, you'll see the lights on—the door blew off in the Nor'easter of '92—and Freddy himself hobbling among the fifty or so Holsteins.

Most folks hoped the big storm in '92 would have put an end to the McHenry farm and are still hoping for some final solution. Not that anyone has anything against Freddy McHenry or small farms—most folks fight to preserve them—but driving by the McHenry farm is a kind of anguish. What holds up the barn has long been a topic of speculation around town, and the house doesn't offer much more assurance. It looks like it might have been a pretty respectable saltbox at one time, but it's been sinking behind one humiliation after another until it is all but hidden behind the collapse of everything else. The fencing is another source of wonder. Where it is and where it isn't, is hard to guess. When you take that long sweeping turn past the farm, you have to keep an eye out for a stray cow that guessed where the fence wasn't. That's the other thing about the McHenry farm. Its bony, carcass-strewn acres spread out on both sides of the main road into town, right after the 'Welcome to Beautiful Galway" sign. It's a dispiriting first impression.

What troubles me most about the farm besides the specter of barn collapsing on cows, a cow and car collision, and the pitiful sight of old Freddy himself, hirsute and hatless, trying to pump life into that 1942 Ford tractor in twenty below, is the one horse remaining.

My friend, Stan, who farmed in Galway most of his life, still knows every farm and hardscrabble farmer left, as well as just about everyone else who comes and goes. Even from a nursing home, he keeps tabs on the town through a social network that still relies on phone and personal visitations. He knew Freddy McHenry and Freddy's father, and he says the McHenry place has been "goin' low" for thirty years, averting total collapse by shifting position from time to time. It is just the McHenry way, he says. Every time Stan tells a story about Freddy McHenry he ends it with a shake of his head and an inward chuckle; I know there is a lot more behind what he knows than he tells, and he tells a lot.

The horse was one of three that Freddy's second wife—and there have been four wives, Stan tells me with a wink—brought to the farm with her. She was an equestrienne, Stan says, stringing out all four syllables. Two of the horses were magnificent 17-hand Friesians, which, after only a month on that windswept rock ledge Freddy calls pasture, looked like the rest of the wreckage up there. When the wife finally ran off she took what remained of her two Friesians with her. The Appaloosa was left behind, just to spite Freddy, some said. Freddy saw no more sense in having a horse than having a cow without teats.

There isn't much for the Appaloosa to hang onto, but he hangs on hard. He's a solid little horse who fits himself into what shelter he can find and survives on what hay spills out of the wagon when Freddy feeds the cows.

Sometimes when I pass the farm, he's up in the pasture, rump to the wind, tail driven between his legs, pawing through snow for anything to eat. On the cruelest January mornings, he'll likely be backed up against the east side of the barn, standing dead still, soaking up the feeble blessing of sun.

As winter slinks away from the McHenry farm, something like life rises up to look around, shifts on its haunches. The wild turkeys creep out of the forest like black-cloaked refugees, picking through the stubble of last year's corn crop. The cows amble out of the barn to make their migration into the muddy pasture in dumb faith that grass will be there. The sun strengthens. The Appaloosa stirs.

Sometimes survival is nonglorious.

WHAT DOESN'T KILL YOU

JAYCEE STOMPED ONE BOOTED FOOT, and then the other, blowing on her red leather gloves. She wasn't exactly dressed for a barn in December, but more for a costume party. It was fashion, I'm sure: equestrienne-themed Victoria's Secret. A short, white, fur jacket over black leathery pants styled after riding breeches. But it was the suede boots that really caught my attention. I couldn't figure how she'd walked up to the barn in them. It seemed like those six-inch, needle-thin heels would pin her into the snow-crusted earth like a tack on a corkboard.

Her car was idling in the driveway, the driver side door open, the interior lit. She'd only been to the barn twice since depositing Mongoose six months earlier; then, only long enough to issue a run-on sentence of instructions before hurrying off. She wasn't staying this time either. Just long enough to inform me that Arvis couldn't count on the board after the end of the month.

"The investors have pulled out," she announced, glancing at the mare pacing in her stall. "We can't afford another breeding fee. We've already shelled out more than we had invested. Breeding," she counted on her gloved fingers, "vet bills, and of course," she added, looking at me sharply, "boarding fees."

I might have urged her to try breeding Mongoose again, but I knew from Marilyn that a mare that conceives twins will probably conceive only twins. Twins seldom go full term and if they do, neither foal will be strong. Besides, I didn't have the heart to think about it. I was still carrying the shocking image of the slipped foals I'd discovered in the pasture. A sight I would not want to see again.

The morning feeding, three days ago. Mongoose trailing afterbirth.

I have handled my share of horse emergencies. The full shock of them happens later; at the time, you do what needs to be done. I settled Mongoose into her stall, called the vet, and then set out in search of what I did not want to find.

It was early April. The temperature had plunged into the teens the night before and the snow-crusted fields glinted hard as steel. I found them in the corner of the galloping field, two heaps of incongruity almost completely obscured by tree shadow. The first one looked mummified, twisted like a gnarled apple-tree branch. It had probably been dead since the first trimester. I followed a splattered trail of dark blood to the second foal. It appeared to have developed normally. I hoped it had been born dead as well. I thought of the word, "slipped." A gentle, fluid word. It did not describe what I was looking at.

"What happens to Mongoose now?"

"I have to move on," Jaycee sighed, adjusting the cylinder of gold bracelets.

"What does that mean?"

She gave me a dismissive look, as if I was too naive to grasp adult matters. "It's business, Mary." Then she paused, sighed, and continued. "This farm is a business, right?"

"Sort of." I grumbled, annoyed by her condescending tone.

"The racing business is *all* business. Not *sort of*—or you lose your shirt." She dug into her red, patent leather bag to retrieve her cell phone, which was blaring "What Doesn't Kill You …"

I could catch a few angrily spit words on Jaycee's end of the conversation. I looked over at Mongoose. The mare had become more agitated, tossing her head and pawing the stall floor. I wondered if she knew we were discussing her future. Whether or not she would have one.

"Sell her as a riding horse," I offered when Jaycee had finally clicked her cell phone closed and dropped it into her bag.

"Sure," she grumbled, her mind still circling the phone conversation.

"I can put the word out. She'd make a beautiful dressage horse with a little training. Someone will take her."

The heels were already clacking across the floor boards, the bracelets jangling. There was an overpowering rush of perfume, heavy as smoke. "If you can do it by the thirtieth," she called over her shoulder. "I'm not paying another month's board."

Her cell phone ringtone sounded again halfway down the slope. It rang out clearly in the still December air. "What Doesn't Kill You," advancing to "makes you stronger" this time, then looping again and again until the car door closed.

I wish the story of Mongoose had another ending, that she had become a champion dressage horse. Someone's tack room decorated with her ribbons. But the life of an ex-race horse only ends that way in fiction.

The evening after the conversation with Jaycee, I stood numbly staring into an empty stall. Though she had not had time to heal from the trauma of the miscarriage, Mongoose had been loaded onto a trailer and taken away sometime after I had come up for the morning chores. Neither Arvis nor I were there to intercede, if we could have.

I called Jaycee's number, but there was no answer. I knew there wouldn't be. Mongoose was most likely on her way to auction. It was business, after all. A clean and clinical solution to what had become a problem. But it was not clean. Mongoose was still in the barn in every way except physically.

I have become familiar with this phenomenon—the afterlife of a horse that has been part of this barn's story. It transforms into another presence. The stall still rung with her agitation. Her halter, with her racing name embossed on a brass nameplate, hung by her stall. In their haste, the truckers had grabbed Angel's halter instead.

And messiest of all was the name plaque that Amanda had made for Mongoose. It had taken several attempts and much consultation. *Mongoose* was painted in streaming letters across the board, using every color Amanda could come up with, some paint, some marker, and then shellacked and sprinkled liberally with glitter. It was Amanda's "thank you" to Mongoose for not harming the kitten that had mysteriously shown up in her stall that day. Whoever had come for Mongoose had removed it from the stall door and tossed it on top of the grain bins. It must have been an irritation to them. They wouldn't know the trick of hitching the door up before sliding it open, and the wooden plaque must have made an aggravating clatter as they tried to wrench the door open.

I hung the plaque back on its hook on the stall door. It would not be clean explaining to Amanda where Mongoose had gone.

After the rescue of Peter Twitch, Amanda and I knew the kitten wasn't in danger of being trampled. Mongoose was not a mean horse. Her rages were all posturing. A defense against a world that one day would find she could not run fast enough.

LASH LARUE

I WAS SURE he wasn't going to show.

This is what my experience with boarders had done: turned me cynical as Arvis. But I had been dragged through the quagmire of disillusionment enough times to earn my cynicism. The ads for boarders had long expired in the local papers when Antonio Banderas called. It sure sounded like him. A soft, rumpled voice explaining that he had a couple of horses he was hoping to board. After Jaycee hijacked Mongoose, Lyla reconciled with her barbarous husband and, to my despair and relief, returned Archie and Viento to their home barn. I had some stalls to fill.

But I'd been here before, in this very spot in fact, standing between the barn's sliding doors looking down the hill toward the drive for a prospective boarder who would never show.

"I'll give him five minutes," I muttered, angry at myself for allowing even a nub of hope, when a black sedan slid up and parked under Shoog. I hadn't seen or heard it turn off the road. I watched in disbelief as a figure emerged from the car and started up to the barn, flickering like a black flame between sunlight and the long reach of afternoon shadow. He was dressed in black. He had black hair. He had green eyes and those eyebrows that start high on the brow and slope down at the ends, giving him a paternal, slightly amused expression. He twinkled when he smiled.

"Mary?" he asked with the spice of an indefinable accent. "We talked on the phone?" I must have looked as dazzled as I was. I fumbled for words, reshuffled some brain cells, and finally spoke. Words were made and, amazingly, they fell into place. I described the farm, the routine, and managed to ask coherent questions.

He had two retired polo ponies in need of a good home. "They're very well trained," he said. "No vices." Then he looked around the farm, breathed in deeply as if he meant to inhale pastures, trees, horses. "It's a beautiful place," he sighed, turning on that blinding smile. "Perfect."

I tried to find my cynicism. Where had it gone so quickly? I needed it to pry open the real story. He must be hiding the horses from an ex-wife or an investor, or looking to dump them somewhere while he fled the country on racketeering charges. But all I could find to ask was, "Do they have any special needs?"

None.

"And I'll be happy to lend a hand when you need me," he added in that voice you wanted to keep on following. He muscled a leaning fence post upright as we talked. He promised to stop by the next day to sign the contract. We shook hands, smiling with mutual delight at the fortuitous transaction. Then he sauntered down the hill.

I never saw him again.

I puzzled over where this phantom man in black had come from and finally concluded that I had invented him. Or resurrected him from my early childhood. He was Lash LaRue, my second cowboy idol, displacing in my affections the wholesome Roy Rogers.

In the late 1950s, I spent a good share of my life nagging, begging, bargaining my way to my aunt and uncle's house on Shelby Island. They were one of the few families I knew with a television set. I even tolerated my cousin Eileen for the thrill of watching Lash LaRue on the Gabby Hayes Show. This was before my Zorro era, and I think Lash LaRue set me up for Zorro and all the men in black I have always been powerfully, disastrously drawn to. It started at age seven, as I sat cross-legged in front of the soccer-ball-sized screen, eating Cheerios with my cousin and watching the adventures of a man in black on a black horse. A little foreign, a little backstreet, cowboy and sophisticate, swinging his hips in synch with his bull whip.

Yep, I made him up. All he had lacked was the whip.

JACKSON AND THE CAT

JACKSON, THE BORDER COLLIE, knows the routine, and his patience with me is true to his tender nature. Each time I come to take care of Daria Symansky's horses, he feels the obligation to show me the routine all over again. But he's very kind about it, never lets on that I'm slow and clumsy and a little stupid.

Daria leaves instructions, an elaborate diagram of the layout of the farm, and details of where to place each horse's grain. There are twelve quarter horses and each has a special need of some sort; none gets the same mixture or portion of grain. Their individual, round, rubber feeders are placed strategically throughout the three-acre field they all share. Two of the horses will only eat side-by-side; others raid any feeder set close to their own; and another old mare must be fed in the run-in shed at the far end of the field. The trick is to maneuver through the herd of hungry horses to dispense the buckets of grain into the individual feeders, and then bully the horses into eating from their own feeders. To Daria this is as routine as brushing her teeth. It never occurs to her that it might not be for me. Jackson is of the same mind as Daria though he tries not to show it. I'm sure he's thinking: *Why don't you know this?*

Bartering horse care is what we do in Galway, so I occasionally get called upon to feed Daria's horses. But I dread it. I dread it the day and night before and during the drive to her farm and only forget to dread it when Jackson darts out from under the junked jeep where he spends the non-working hours of the day. Jackson and I only see one another two or three times a year, but we have a bond. Before I do anything, I hug Jackson; then, he puts his head in my lap and I run my hands over his exquisite little head and tell him how I've missed him and what a good, brave dog he is. It's like a prayer ritual, or whatever football players do before the start of a game. We both need that moment. Then Jackson lifts his head, pricks his ears. It's time for work. He leads me into the grain shed and I measure out the portions of grain into buckets and place them in the handcart.

Measuring out grain and loading it into the cart takes too long for Jackson, who starts up to the field repeatedly only to return and regard me with a rather condescending cock of his head.

"Hold on, Jackson. I don't do this every day," I remind him. He wags his tail forgivingly. I could add that I do, by the way, know the way up to the field, but showing me the way is one of Jackson's pleasures.

I follow him up the hill, pulling the cart of twelve buckets with their individual grain mixtures. The horses are jostling one another at the gate like they're ready to charge through, which I fear they will do if I try to enter that way. Carrying four buckets of grain at a time, I slip between the fence rails and dash to fill the buckets. Back and forth I go, dodging and weaving like a running back. The horses are whirling and spinning in a feeding frenzy, but they're not my only problem. It's Jackson. He thinks he needs to herd them.

The horses don't need herding; in fact, they resent being herded by a skinny collie, bred to boss around sheep. But herd Jackson must. He circles, charges, nips ankles, yanks on tails. He is a swarm of mosquitoes. The horses swat at him with swishing tails, lunges, and kicks, and I'm in the midst of it all. Caught in a skirmish of horse flesh, I dump grain willy-nilly, having no idea who's getting what. Throwing the last of the empty buckets ahead of me, I dive for the fence.

Only after the horses decide to ignore him and settle down to eat is Jackson satisfied he has them where he wants them. Then, hearing the siren call of duty, he's off again, whizzing around the perimeter of the pasture, a blur of black and white. This time, he's rounding up imaginary strays. Gradually, he narrows his circle, driving the phantom horses back into the herd.

When the horses saunter away from their feeders to munch contentedly on hay, Jackson's work is done. He waits for me with head cocked, while I fill the mangers with hay and load the empty buckets back on the cart.

But this is where Jackson's herd-dog bravado slips. THE CAT, up until now sleeping away in the dog house from which he long ago ejected Jackson, stalks up to meet us. Jackson, timid, sweet, deluded, is terrified of THE CAT. I see this immediately in THE CAT's swagger, the malicious tail twitch. He's not a big cat—some scrawny stray dropped off at Daria's farm years ago—but he's got attitude. He intercepts Jackson on the path going down to the shed and for a moment there's a standoff. Jackson attempts to pass; THE CAT leaps in front of him; Jackson jigs the other way; THE CAT parlays his move. This mirror game goes on for a few seconds, THE CAT savoring Jackson's humiliation, until Jackson finally leaps over THE CAT and escapes to the shed. I pretend I don't see a thing.

Back at the shed, Jackson watches me with a woebegone expression as I put away the buckets and cart, lock up the shed. Meanwhile, THE CAT is settled at his dinner bowl, awaiting his and Jackson's meal. THE CAT always eats first, and then samples Jackson's kibble before Jackson has a mouthful. I don't interfere with this hierarchy because it only makes things worse for Jackson. We have an understanding: None of it happens.

While THE CAT is eating, I say my goodbyes to Jackson, running my hands over his head and looking into his soulful eyes. I tell him again what a good, brave dog he is. "But, Jackson," I whisper, "what you need is sheep."

RESCUES

YOU KNOW RIGHT AWAY—from his swollen joints to the leery cast of his eyes—that Ozzy has not been kindly treated. But his rescuer could match him for hard-luck stories. Rosie has bad knees and a bad back, and unlike Ozzy, she's still working. Also, unlike Ozzy, Rosie expects the best of people, at least until proven otherwise.

Ozzy has known only the worst. He is a veteran barrel racer that was literally run into the ground. A well-bred palomino gelding, he must have been a handsome guy at one time. He still has a little machismo left, enough to spark the mares into heat on occasion. But mostly, Ozzy just wants to be left alone—by horses and people—to live out his days grazing or dozing at the farthest end of the pasture, or parked over his own pile of hay.

Marilyn used to say she wasn't running an orphan camp, but she did take in horses in desperate circumstance, at least temporarily. Arvis, to my surprise, allowed Rosie to board Ozzy at the farm for about half the usual boarding fee. The old horse doesn't ask much. He could probably get by in an alleyway. Rosie says he spent his life packed in pens with twenty other horses at rodeo events or stuck in the back of a trailer. When she rescued him from the slaughter pen, she had to keep him in the mud patch of her mother's yard until she found the Rumsley farm.

Ozzy has never known pasture. He must think he's in heaven here. If so, his gratitude isn't evident. He comes in and out of the barn for feedings with the resignation of an inmate, and spends his days as far away from the other horses as possible. I wish he'd at least give a nicker of recognition to Rosie, who has chronic back and hip pain, and has spent a good share of what she makes from two minimum-wage jobs to pay his board and vet bills.

It has been my experience that people who rescue horses usually need rescue themselves. Rosie, for example. She's been on her own since she was fourteen and has been smacking into dead-end jobs and relationships ever since. I've heard snatches of her story, but frankly, I try not to know too much. Boarders can suck you into the pity pit quickly, and I've been there once too often. Not that Rosie expects pity or anything else she doesn't earn herself. She accepts her disabilities and defeats as if they are members of her dysfunctional family. She'll laugh about them sooner than complain. But when I watch her hobble down from the barn toward her 1988 VW strung together with wire and electrical tape, my heart aches for her. How, I wonder, does she make it home, let alone through the next day?

I wonder the same about Ozzy. Each day when I call the horses in for their grain, he's the last to answer, trudging in from the pasture as if he is hauling the remainder of the day with him, one ponderous step following another. During his barrel-racing days he was spurred to sudden bursts of speed, turns, and skidding stops. Nothing can spur him now. He takes his time. I half expect when I call him into the barn for the morning and after-noon feedings that he will have decided he is done answering.

Today might be that day. The other horses are long into the barn, but no Ozzy. Finally, I see him break away from the shadows of the hedge row and start his unhurried migration toward the barn. I wait for what seems ten minutes for his arrival. When he is just feet away from entering the barn, he stops. Something snares his slumbering attention in the galloping field to his left. His head flies up, nostrils flare. Then Ozzy takes off.

I'm not worried. Ozzy is almost thirty, severely arthritic, and not given to flighty notions. I sigh and wait for the will and wind to fail. But as I watch, his intentions seem to amplify, even as his figure recedes into the distance. His gait lengthens, becomes rhythmic and effortless until he is a flicker of bronze and gold, heading for the galloping field which seems to wait for him, holding the last light of the day.

RIDING LESSON

REGINA, PETER TWITCH, AND I wait in the doorway of the barn, watching as the two girls approach. Though we don't speak of it, something has changed between them. They are going in different directions now. Only one seems to know it.

Tina runs ahead of Amanda, ignoring whatever Amanda is saying, breathlessly, behind her. Amanda is so focused on Tina she does not even stop to acknowledge Peter Twitch, who has, in his customary fashion, come to greet and escort her into the barn.

Tina wants to get into the saddle. As usual, she is impatient with the grooming, and today Amanda is too. Angel is alert to her anxiety. She nudges Amanda with her muzzle to get her attention, but Amanda is too busy trying to keep Tina in her sights. It's a lost cause. Tina is in the saddle already and heading out to the riding ring. Amanda yanks at the girth, trying to tighten it in one attempt. Angel lays back her ears and bumps her in reprimand.

"Gradually, Amanda," Regina steps in and loosens the girth. "You know that." Amanda does, of course. She lowers her head, nods. Regina watches while Amanda leads Angel into the riding ring and walks her in circles, stops, tightens the girth a little, walks on before tightening it again. All the while Amanda's eyes are following Tina who is cantering circles around her.

Tina urges Trixster into flying lead changes. I can't find it in my heart to praise her adequately, though she keeps twirling around in the saddle to face me, waving, smiling expectantly. I'm irked at her pageantry of horsemanship, while Amanda struggles to launch herself into the saddle, an undertaking that never happens in a single motion.

Regina and I watch as Amanda kicks Angel immediately into the trot. Regina sighs. Today, Amanda is not Amanda, but neither Regina nor I interfere with the little drama taking place. It's the last gasp of a friendship and it's hard to watch.

In the ring, Tina pushes Trixster into a brisk trot, and Amanda, who is usually content at a walk or slow trot, urges Angel to keep up. I can see Regina is uneasy with this, as Amanda seems to have forgotten everything she's been taught. She leans too far forward, her weight shifted over Angel's withers, and each post is a pounding. Angel is indignant. Her ears are flattened and her back rigid. Regina steps in front of them and takes the reins from Amanda, easing Angel back to a walk. Amanda crumples over the saddle. Tina flies by ignoring her.

Both Regina and I are relieved when the lesson is over and the girls have left the barn, Tina running ahead to the car and Amanda far behind, not trying to keep up now. I'm a little afraid that Tina's mother will drive off without Amanda, for neither she nor her daughter like to allow a moment to drop between activities. Amanda, head down and feet dragging, is definitely making them wait, even while Tina bounces in the back seat and yells out the window at her and Tina's mother stares fixedly ahead. I know this is a form of protest for Amanda, the only one left to her.

By the time Amanda reaches them, Tina is outside the car, holding the door open, still bouncing, still yelling. Amanda climbs into the back seat. Tina slams the door behind her and hops into the front seat next to her mother.

Regina and I watch them drive off. We both know it is the last riding lesson the two girls will be taking together. And it will be a long time before we see Amanda again.

NORMA ROGERS

TINA TOOK HER LESSON alone after that, and Amanda, as we feared, didn't come at all. She'd lost her friend and her ride. When I asked Tina if she'd seen Amanda, she shrugged and looked away. Tina brought other friends to the barn occasionally, mostly to show off her riding skills. But I doubt they were friends in the same way she and Amanda had been. We only have a friend like that once.

Mine was Norma Rogers. I was eleven when my family moved to Puget Sound, and Norma lived next door in an identical cedar-sided house perched on stilts on the hillside. We had much in common. We were both tragically misunderstood and underappreciated by our families, and we worshipped horses. We drew horses, read all the Walter Farley novels, created our own horse dramas, stalked anyone who rode a horse by us on the beach. We were both mind-blown over Zorro, but more than Zorro, we coveted his black horse, Tornado.

I can see the two of us sitting atop the bulkhead between our two houses, swinging goop-booted feet in the air, staring across the sound to Vashon Island. We never made arrangements to meet, we simply found ourselves together at the same time in the same place. Like gulls, one of us would appear on the bulkhead; soon after, the other would alight beside her. There would be some affront to pick over, or another incident in which one of our many talents was misinterpreted. What our many talents were, I am not sure, but they included sole spearing, tag, hopscotch, and horsemanship. Horsemanship was mostly illusionary, since our experience with horses had been limited to the movie screen and books.

Eventually our many hours spent on the bulkhead led to the big plan. It went something like this: We would skip high school, knowing pretty much everything worthwhile anyway, and take off for Wyoming to start our own horse ranch. There were details to work out, not least of which was the color of the horses we would round up to start our ranch. There would have to be a black, of course. A Tornado.

Like Amanda, I stayed in the dream while my friend grew out of it. Junior high school had a profound effect on Norma. Her voice became higher pitched, she laughed too much, and her sentences curled up at the ends. She was no longer my serious, thoughtful, horse-besotted friend. She had gone downright goofy. And she acquired even goofier friends. They would huddle together in a plume of over-teased hair and talk in excited whispers. I was definitely excluded from Norma's crowd and it hurt like a toothache.

One day, perhaps out of the same desperation Amanda felt in losing Tina, I approached the cluster of friends at Norma's locker. I wasn't sure what I was going to say to them and was more surprised than anyone when I blurted out the long abandoned plan that Norma and I had once talked about to exhaustion. I told all, right down to the color of the horses. A bewildered silence followed. Norma just looked at me standing there on the sandbar of my isolation with the tide coming in. Then she and the bundle of girls turned on their heels and fled down the hall, giggling moronically.

I don't remember if I ever spoke to Norma after that. If I went down to the bulkhead with my angst, she never followed. I hated her, missed her, loved her. And I still do, a little.

So here's to first friendships, the ones that happen without the integument of self-protection or restraint. The tender, vulnerable, unrestrained openness that is only once.

THE SUMMER OF THE MOVIE PEOPLE

MARILYN HAD A FLINTY PERSONALITY. The slightest provocation could ignite a conflagration. Outside of Liberals, nothing struck her ire like trespassers—whether on her property or on her way of doing things. Arvis used to tell the story about the day, wielding a pitchfork, she cornered a turkey hunter who had rashly ignored the No Trespassing signs posted along the farm's property lines. After her death, Arvis didn't tell that story anymore, thinking, I guess, it wasn't respectful of her memory. But that story was Marilyn in a teacup, and it charmed Arvis, though he'd probably never admit it.

So the summer of the movie people would have been the summer of Marilyn's life. I can see her bristling and glinting and setting off in all directions, her voice zapping every living thing off its feet. But the movie people did not descend upon the Rumsley farm until the second summer after Marilyn had passed away. Marilyn missed her finest moment.

Who would have thought such a thing would happen in Galway? Who would have thought Arvis would have any part of it? But Arvis had become a man of surprises. After all, I thought he'd be happy to be out of the horse business, shed of the farm, and off on his fishing skiff scouring the coast of Maine for sea bass. What he never saw any sense in, which included a lot, suddenly seemed to settle in a new light.

Typically, Arvis let out the news like smoke rings.

He ambled into the barn one morning in May while I was mucking out stalls. Without offering a word, he leaned on the half wall separating the middle barn and the mulch hay bay and chewed on the stem of the pipe

Marilyn had long ago made impotent. Arvis seldom paid social calls to the barn due to his allergies and dislike for horses, so I knew this visit had a purpose. I didn't want to hear what it was. The farm was leaking money, and we were down to three horses again with no potential boarders on the horizon. I knew Arvis' family had amped up their campaign for him to sell the farm and move to Schenectady. The farm would be prime pickings for a developer. My heart did a little stutter-step each time I thought about that. So I kept mucking out stalls, ignoring Arvis for as long as possible.

"It's going to be a little different around here," he said at last. I straightened up, sighed, and gave him my wary attention. But what he told me in his slow, phlegmatic way, studying the stem of his pipe as if divining his words from it, wasn't anything I could have expected. The farm, he droned, as if relating the state of the weather, was to be the location for an independent film. "Movie people," as he referred to them, had approached him the week before with the proposition. They found the farm after scouting Upstate New York for a couple of years for the right location for their film. It had to be "vintage," he said. With Marilyn no longer cracking the whip on Arvis, the farm had turned the corner on vintage and was zeroing in on decline.

Oh, and it seemed horses were an important component of the storyline. When asked if there were, in fact, "lots of horses" on the farm, Arvis, to whom a lot of horses was one horse, assured them there were.

While Arvis was telling me all this, I tried to envision his initial encounter with the movie people. I imagined them slipping out of a Lexus or perhaps a Cadillac limo in their pointy shoes and pointy hair. Their voices would arch and twine as they explained to Arvis—who would be prone beneath his recalcitrant tractor—their fantastical proposition. They must have sounded like shamans to him. I wished I could have been there when Arvis scooted out from underneath the tractor and set on them the look I knew so well. It was a look of puzzlement that screwed up his entire

face, and said, indubitably, this is not a man who brooked nonsense. But I can't see what happened after that. Can't imagine it. Somehow a deal was struck, a contract signed. A movie crew was going to work their cinematic magic on the Rumsley farm. That would mean major renovations to the house, barn, and property to shape it to their purpose. Arvis would pass the summer in Maine.

"It's in your hands," he said as if it was a matter of remembering to bring in the mail. What "in your hands" meant exactly, I had no way of knowing. But I couldn't help but be excited about the idea of a film being made on the farm. Maybe I'd be in it. Maybe the Rumsley farm would become famous, a tourist destination with boarders beckoning from all corners of the state. Fences repaired, the back door of the barn finally set straight on its track, the intractable stall doors corrected, fresh paint, the run-in shed roof finally replaced, halters with gold embossed name plates for the horses. I couldn't wait to tell Ken, to tell the town of Galway!

"Oh," Arvis added, pulling the pipe out of his mouth. "They're independent. Don't pay union scale, so they want to keep the whole thing quiet as they can." I must have looked thunderstruck because he made his point even stronger. "Don't tell anyone. *Anyone.*"

Don't tell anyone?

If the movie people weren't quite what I imagined them to be, they were every bit as alien. There were more of them than I expected, and each one came with a title: script directors and location directors and lighting directors and prop directors. It went on and on. When the actual director arrived, I barely caught a glimpse of him. He reminded me of a queen bee, with all the lesser directors and workers clustering around, moving as he moved, allowing only a small pocket of personal space. I watched the hive of directors move from house to barn and back again until the director finally broke free and escaped in a rented Jeep.

All the movie people came with rented Jeeps and L.L. Bean flannel shirts. They lost the flannel shirts once July heat set in. Then they darted about in tank tops, shorts, and flip flops, flapping at mosquitoes and stable flies. As I watched them flit and scurry about the property, I realized they were not at all equipped for the visceral world that required long pants and sturdy shoes. It was kind of fun watching them scratch and slap and complain to one another. It was their only humanizing quality. They were otherwise too perfect. Sculpted and sleek as steel. They didn't make eye contact.

After the initial meeting with the location director, Arvis packed up and left for Maine with nary an instruction thrown back in my direction. I was to "consult" with—meaning, I was under the direction of—the location director and prop director. This rankled a bit, which the directors sensed, I guess, because they quickly offered me an appeasing title: locale consultant. I am ashamed to say how easily I was taken in by that silly title. But even

Marilyn would have been defused by this bunch. She could handle any situation as long as it came at her straight on, but the movie people didn't operate that way. They writhed around you like a constrictor.

I had it all wrong about the "renovations" the movie people would make to the property—the back door would not be righted, the fences would not be called to attention, the stall doors would remain recalcitrant. What the movie people were attracted to about the Rumsley place was how easily it could concede to abject abandonment. They removed a few boards from the barn, blackened windows, and antiqued the house and barn siding a gothic shade of gray wash. But when they, or rather their work crew, began removing fence rails, I had to step in. "There *are* horses here," I reminded them. There needed to be at least an appearance of confinement.

"Horses," mused the location director, to whom I had been hastily introduced. His name was Win or Fin or Rin. "Where?" he asked. Apparently, Angel, Trixster, and Ozzy were easily overlooked as they had retreated to the back pastures since the invasion of the movie people.

"We have horses," I huffed. "Three of them."

"Three?" The prop director, Syd, approached, wrinkling a brow that may never have been wrinkled before. This was clearly a consternation. "I thought you had lots of horses," he gasped, looking around the pastures as if horses might surely appear. "We need *lots* of horses," he insisted, growing agitated. He had somehow overlooked a prop essential to the storyline. "Where can we get them?" he asked the locale consultant, suddenly aware of my existence.

"I have an ad for boarders running in the local paper," I said defensively, "but the way you people have trashed the place ..."

"We'll rent them!" Syd waved his hands dismissively. I noticed for the first time that, except for his eyebrows, Syd was completely hairless. He scanned the pastures again as if he might have missed the horse-rental kiosk. He pursed his lips and turned to me. "Where?"

I pondered the question. "Well, I could ask the neighbors to lend us their horses for awhile." Syd clasped his hands together ecstatically. Then, a thought slithered into my mind. "But I'd have to charge board ..."

"Whatever," intruded Win or Fin or Rin impatiently as he smacked a stable fly off his pink calf. Then, remembering to treat me with that smooth, meringue-sweet condescension he seemed to think worked so well on us back-country folk, purred, "I'm sure you could arrange it."

"Of course," I said. Then, before he and Syd could waft away on the next wave of urgent business, "but I'll have to tell them why ..."

Of course there was no way that Galway wasn't going to find out about the invasion of the movie people, regardless. News travels like blight. You don't know where it starts and you can't stop it. The news had set in by the time I approached the farms at the four corners. It wasn't necessary for me to rehearse, over and over again, a convincing tale to entice the Logans to board their horses at the Rumsley farm for the rest of the summer. They offered their horses up before I got through the prologue. I probably didn't have to tell them their names would be included in the credits.

"Credits?" They became tremulous at the mention of the word.

"Of course ... you and your horses!" I could feel myself being sucked into their excitement. "Maybe you'll even be in the movie," I added, "as extras. I could talk to the director." Of course I hadn't even been introduced to the director.

The idea of being in a movie has a powerful effect on people. Even Janine Logan and her husband, Frank, who are almost as prosaic as Arvis, unmoved by any flummery that blows their way, were caught up in movie fever.

"Will there be lines?" Janine asked a little breathlessly. Before I could answer, she clasped my hand, eyes widening, "And will I be riding? Do they give you a riding outfit to wear or ..."

"I think extra means you don't have to worry about all that." I was becoming worried about what I had stupidly set in motion.

"But we *will* be in the movie?"

"As I say, I'll talk to the director."

"And credits … there will be credits?"

"Yes, yes, credits." We were all nodding our heads in unison. "For the horses, too," I added.

No one seemed to remember that this was a small, independent film. It had become the Titanic. More people were climbing on board by the day. The McClellans had agreed to have the hulk of a DeSoto exhumed from their hedgerow to enhance the impression of decrepitude to the Rumsley yard. The Wileys were mowing the back pasture for the staging trailers to be parked, and several of the locals, including Kyle, the high school kid who helped with haying, were hired to do grunt work. The directors would not lift anything heavier than their sunglasses off their noses. They carried only smart phones and clipboards. They issued instructions—not orders, they were quick to remind us—and guidance.

Even Butch and Wally's Used Ladder World got in on the action. I spied Butch on one of their ladders blackening a kitchen window while Wally hurled insults up at him. They seemed to be doing a good job making the place look worse. It fell within their skill set.

The place hummed with energy. My reservations were cancelled out by the promise of income for the farm and, probably more seductively, the chance for Angel to have a featured role in the movie. I had talked Syd into considering her for the role of the horse the child actor, yet to be named, would be grooming in one of the scenes. Angel was patient with children, I insisted, and extremely photogenic. I spent hours grooming her for her scene, trimmed and oiled her hooves. Polished her up like a carousel pony. She would be ready when the call came.

Meanwhile, the farm was fast slipping from a state of moderate neglect into terminal shabbiness as the movie people transformed house and barn, fences and fields into what they needed them to be. It was in my hands, Arvis had said, but really very little was. There were thirty people at a time swarming the property, shouting orders, checking devices, brandishing clipboards, looking frazzled, though well coiffed. I gave up any pretence of control and concentrated on how to get Angel's tail to look like the rest of her. It was less than ample, her tail; barely adequate, actually. When she was in heat, it shot straight up in the air like a flag pole, minus the flag. And there was the problem of the Logans. I'd led them to believe they would be extras and yet there had been no mention among the many directors about extras. I hoped to get a chance to pose this question to Win-Fin-Rin, but he was as hard to catch as a barn cat. Which, by the way, had vanished either into the recesses of the hay mow or into the woods. But no worry. Syd had ordered more.

I was looking for Win-Fin-Rin with the question of extras in mind when I glimpsed something foreign standing against the half wall. I would not have been surprised by a director studying an angle for a scene, but Amanda seemed out of place. She looked at me, then around the barn as if she had stepped through a breach in reality and didn't know the way back.

"Amanda? What are you doing here?" Because she did, indeed, seem out of context.

"Ticks," she answered weakly.

"Ticks?" I repeated. I hadn't seen Amanda since the riding lessons. I'd forgotten about checking for ticks. I'd forgotten about Amanda.

"Trixster gets them worst," she reminded me, starting for the back door with a bag of carrots in her hand.

"Oh, not now, Amanda," I said. "Trixster's being shot! I mean, they're taking shots of the horses in the pasture."

Amanda did not look like this made any sense. She hadn't been at the barn since before the invasion and, apparently, was the only person in Galway who didn't have a part in the movie. I hastily explained about the film crew, the changes to the farm, my new title, the new barn cats soon to arrive, Angel's premiere role in the movie. Amanda looked skeptical, her fingers nervously plucking at a hay bale.

"Don't touch that." I snapped before I could stop myself. "They're very particular about … the smallest thing," I trailed off.

"Is it going to stay like this?" She looked from the missing boards in the siding up into the hay mow with its artfully positioned hay bales, rearranged from Arvis' precision stacks for a more casual, tumbled-down look. Syd blew by without a look in our direction. She watched him go with an expression of scowling bewilderment. The same look I'd seen on her face when analyzing some foreign body plucked out of one of the horse's coats.

I explained that everything would be put back the way it was but this didn't seem to reassure her much. She walked into Angel's stall and looked out the window into the field. The horses were at the farthest corner, grazing near the hedgerow, ignoring the man following them with a camera. Seeing Amanda silhouetted in the window, holding a bag of carrots, I remembered that I missed her. I missed the barn, the cats, the horses, even the routine, as they had been—set in reality. I wanted to run out to the back door with her and call the horses in. Then Win-Fin-Rin appeared, looking this way and that, probably in pursuit of Syd.

"Wait," I yelled, and chased him with my question about extras.

As it turned out, I didn't have to worry about getting the Logans a part. Or about Angel's skimpy tail. The movie people and all the expectations and chaos they brought with them vanished as quickly as barn swallows after the fledging of the last brood. All that chattering and swoop just gone.

It's not that I didn't see it coming. About the time the actors were scheduled to arrive and filming to begin, there was a drop in air pressure. The energy shifted from everyone everywhere and digital and shouted commands cross hatching the airways, to groups of directors huddled in hushed conversations. They scattered at my approach. Gradually their ranks thinned, until there was only Win-Fin-Rin. He ran his palm over the flip of hair at his forehead and announced to the bewildered locals that the movie was in "suspension." They could all go home until summoned. They looked to me for explanations. But the directors weren't talking to me.

When I called Arvis to report all this, it wasn't news to him. He had been in contact with the movie people all along. He explained to me that the lead actor for the film had been offered another role and reneged on his contract. With his defection, the film's investors pulled out of the project. "Happens all the time," Arvis said as if he was now an aficionado of the film industry. "These independent films … half of them don't get made."

"But the farm …" I protested. "It looks like something out of "Tobacco Road."

"They have to put it back as they found it," Arvis said. "And they have to compensate the farm for every cent we agreed to. Film or no film. It's in the contract." Arvis seemed quite pleased with himself. "I get a brand new Kubota out of it!"

"But … what about …" I wasn't sure how to articulate the gap in reality that was flapping in the wind. The quantity of wasted money was staggering to me. All that had been spent on directors, staff, work on the property, props. The barn cat rental alone was five hundred dollars, which Win-Fin-Rin had casually dropped one day.

"Cost of doing business," Arvis said.

By September it was as if the movie people had never been. The clean-up crew—a new set of workers I hadn't seen before—swept in, and within three days had remade what had been unmade. The sidings of house and barn returned to their original on the brink of, but not quite there, state of decline. The windows were replaced, the hay restacked, the imported barn cats packed up and sent onto their next assignment, the neighbors' horses returned to their own pastures, the Logans and the other locals' dreams of stardom dashed. The pastures were overgrown and thick with thistles, burdocks, wild parsnip. But Arvis could take care of that when he returned from Maine and picked out his new Kubota.

It took awhile for the normal pitch of life on the farm to find itself again. The swallows had migrated; the turkeys resumed their parades across the fields. The horses grazed closer to the barn. The native barn cats resettled in the mow, the season progressed toward fall, and Amanda returned.

The last I had seen of her was that day two weeks before, when I had left her standing bewildered in Angel's stall while I pursued Win-Fin-Rin. By the time I remembered to look for her, she was a distant figure heading south on Parkis Mills Road, too far away to call back. I'd thought of her often since then, but didn't know how to get in touch with her. In all the time I had known Amanda, she'd never given me a phone number, and her living arrangements seemed conditional. For all I knew, she had moved away again.

I was filling the water tank when I caught sight of a small figure on a bicycle struggling up Parkis Mills Road. I hung up the hose and hurried to the front door of the barn and followed her progress to the driveway, up the driveway, until she parked the bicycle, another clattering carcass, under Shoog. The missing piece of the landscape was finally set back in place. I watched as she made her way up the slope, head down. She might not have looked up at all except that Peter Twitch came out to greet her, calling in his raspy voice. Amanda fell on her knees to gather him up. For awhile she was so absorbed in stroking and talking to Peter Twitch, it seemed that was all she had come for. Finally she looked up and gave a little tentative wave.

"I've been waiting for you!" I shouted. She smiled self-consciously and remained sitting in the grass cradling Peter Twitch who was being uncharacteristically tolerant of the excessive attention. She seemed perfectly happy where she was, sure, at least, of Peter Twitch's welcome.

"I think there are kittens in the hay mow," I said after awhile. She looked up. "I can hear them, but can't get to them."

She released Peter Twitch and, with a shuffling of knees and elbows, got to her feet. When she reached me standing in the doorway, she squinted up at me, shrugged and hurried past. Amanda was never one for unnecessary words. I watched her climb the stairs to the mow and crouch there like an Abinaki scout, listening. Hearing what I did not hear, she began realigning hay bales. Then she tunneled out of sight. I waited for a few minutes, then I climbed the stairs after her.

I could hear muffled grunts, gasps for air, and the thump and shift of hay bales. Then silence. "How's it coming?" No answer.

After a few minutes in which I imagined Amanda asphyxiated, crushed beneath an avalanche of hay bales, I heard the familiar underground babble of her voice.

"You must have found them," I called. Within a few minutes she emerged from the mountain of hay bales, her face flushed red, spider webs netting her hair, and hay sticking to her sweated cheeks. She held three kittens—two tigers and one black. She handed the black one to me. And smiled. A rare and wonderful thing, and I laughed with the delight of it. "You're back, Amanda!" She turned self-conscious again, clutched the two kittens to her chest, and made her way down the stairs. I followed with the black kitten clinging to my shoulder with his tiny but effective claws piercing through my sweatshirt.

"I think they're old enough to eat canned food," Amanda announced. I fetched the last can in the tack room, popped it open, and divided it into the two cat dishes. We placed the kittens down in front of them. After a few tentative sniffs they plunged with all paws into the cat food, growling menacingly.

"How long do you think the mother's been gone?" Amanda asked, looking down at the gnashing, growling kittens.

"Long enough for them to be very, very hungry. You found them just in time, Amanda. I never would have been able to get to them."

Amanda shrugged, grinned.

For a long time we sat watching the kittens, chuckling at their personality shifts from voracious to vulnerable. There was so much to catch up on and so much more I wanted to say to Amanda. I wanted to tell her how much I had missed her, even if it hadn't seemed that way, how the barn wasn't the same without her. But I would have to find another way. Amanda wasn't into hyperbole.

"What should we name them?" Amanda asked, sitting cross-legged on the barn floor, gazing down at the three kittens as if they were something miraculous, something never seen before.

"How about Tornado for this one," I said, lifting the black kitten into my lap. "What do you think?"

HORSES MAKE A LANDSCAPE

AS A KID, I LOVED WESTERNS. Horses were indestructible in westerns, capable of tumbling head over heel, fording rivers, breaking through fences, stampeding over cliffs, and always rebounding, popping up again and again to carry on at a gallop in double time. I didn't know about the trip wires which regularly killed or crippled stunt horses back then. Often the horse that emerged from a devastating fall was not the horse that went down. Horses were trained to go against their nature, often at the cost of their lives.

I cringe when I see those movies now. It's not only the falls that horses were forced into, but the brutality of the horsemanship. The horse was an extension of the cowboy machismo. If an actor had a sharp line to deliver, he underscored it with a savage yank of the reins and kick to the ribs. The horse was spurred into rearing and bucking, or breaking into a dead gallop from a standstill. The horse was theatrical. Without the horse, a cowboy was just a bow-legged man with a gun.

Horses weren't props in the real West. They were necessities of survival, being not only the means of transportation but the bulk of the work force. The pioneers who settled the West staked their lives on getting the horse to do what needed doing, and—since sound horses were not so easy to come by—doing it for as long as possible. People who depended upon horses knew their frailties as well as their strengths and respected the limits of their big hearts and willingness to serve.

These days horses are out of work for the most part. Even in the movie stunt scenes, horses and their actions can be digitally generated so what you see is pure illusion. No horse need apply. Angel and Trixster are under saddle just often enough to earn the status of saddle horses; Mongoose's job was to give birth to a future stakes winner to fulfill her owners' fantasy; Viento and Archie were what Marilyn used to call "pasture ornaments;" Ozzy basks in retirement; and Margie, the latest boarder, mostly serves as a symbol of a life her owner hopes to have.

Eve's struggle to pay Margie's board is epic. All I know of Eve's back story is that she has "difficulties," her explanation for why the board is always late or short. But I don't need details to see how hard her life is. Eve seems ever braced for something heavy to fall on her. Her visits to the barn are snatched between stints of work and hardships. I won't see her for weeks; then, as I'm waiting for the water tank to fill, I might catch sight of her car pulled over on Parkis Mills Road, just where I used to stop to gaze upon the barn before I became a part of it. She will be leaning against the fence line, looking out toward the horses grazing in the pasture. One windy day last month, I watched as she slipped through the fence rails with the agility of a girl, and rushed up to Margie. The mare—startled at first—lowered her head in welcome. Even from a distance, I could see the tenderness that passed between the two as they leaned together into one shadow.

Knowing how hard it was for her to pay Margie's board, I once suggested to Eve that she consider selling the horse. But Eve was adamant. She would never sell Margie. I didn't bring it up again.

Last week, I was surprised to find Eve at the barn when I came to do the evening chores. She and Amanda were grooming Margie on cross-ties. The tone of Eve's voice as she swirled the curry comb through Margie's coat was free flowing and sparkling as running sap. She was demonstrating for Amanda how to work the winter out of a horse's coat. They must have been at it a long time. Dust and horse hair flew around in shafts of sunlight and coated the head and shoulders of Eve and Amanda and even found its way

to Peter Twitch, perched on the half wall and looking on with grave interest, as if the grooming of a horse was the most fascinating thing he had ever seen.

I watched as intently as Amanda and Peter Twitch while Eve selected a brush to finish the job, and within a few strokes had raised, from the midden of winter, a gleaming bay coat. Each stroke of the brush seemed to loosen something in Eve. Finally, running her hand over Margie's glossy shoulder, she turned to Amanda with a smile long buried, yet quick to find its way. "Isn't she beautiful," she beamed.

If horses are no more than illusion these days, they're a necessary one. As Lame Deer, the Sioux Seeker of Visions said, "Horses make a landscape more beautiful."

SHIT-KICKER

SUSAN HURRIED UP THE SLOPE toward the barn in a flurry of chiffon and various dangling accessories. Her thirteen-year-old, Farrell, in new riding breeches and shiny black riding boots, slumped beside her. Farrell was coming for her first riding lesson, something she had no more interest in doing than in learning the polka.

"She's always loved horses," Susan gushed. "She can't wait to get started." I wondered which of the two Susan was really referring to.

I had bartered riding lessons for haircuts. Susan was the local hairdresser, school-bus driver, Pilates instructor, and realtor. I had agreed to the riding lessons for her daughter thinking I could bargain with Regina to take them over in exchange for horse care. Sadly, Regina and her family were in the midst of a move, leaving me holding the reins, so to speak.

I didn't have to worry. The riding lessons did not last beyond the third visit when Trixster, sensing the rider's malaise, decided to match and raise it. Even Susan had to admit it was like trying to pump air into a punctured inflatable.

I was off the hook and Susan had done her best to give her daughter an authentic, rather than virtual, life experience. Something to check off the good-parenting column for whomever tallies these things up.

I did not expect to see Susan billowing up the hill toward the barn the next Monday afternoon.

"Surprised to see me?" she asked breathlessly.

I was. And bewildered by her offer to help with barn chores.

"I know I don't have any experience," she quickly added, "but I can sweep and comb hair and fill the tanks and put out the straw or whatever it is they eat."

"Actually, Susan, I have lots of help," I lied.

"I could do something ..." She looked down at the tiny scenes painted on her inch-long nails. She was next to tears.

God, save me. "We can try it and see," I mumbled.

She looked like she had just received benediction. "Can we start now?"

"Uh ... no," I nodded in the direction of her sequined flip-flops. "They don't work in a barn." Nothing about Susan worked in a barn. "Think of it as a reverse dress code," I said. "Whatever you usually wear, don't."

I envisioned Susan slogging through springtime mud, shoveling manure out of the run-in sheds. This wouldn't last as long as the riding lessons.

Like old barns, people have understories. They are seldom who they appear to be on the surface. Horses know this immediately. We humans take longer. Sometimes we need it standing right before our eyes—like Susan, red faced and blue nosed, on a March morning, two degrees, in muck boots, canvas overalls, and a bomber hat, hacking at hillocks of frozen manure. Beneath the fashions, poofy hair, and manicured nails is what my friend, Stanley, would have called a "shit kicker," his highest praise.

While I thought the novelty would wear off within a week or two, Susan took on barn chores like another of her vocations. She arrived every Friday and Sunday morning, through the worst that all seasons could bring. And once the threat of riding lessons was lifted, Farrell joined her on Sunday mornings. Turns out, Farrell loved horses, just not riding them. She liked to sit in the hay mow and draw horses and cats.

It took me awhile to accept that Susan was an authentic shit-kicker. Once winter came, and a heavy snow was predicted, I told Susan she shouldn't come to the barn. Dangerous driving, cold, misery, etc. "In fact," I said, "you shouldn't come at all during the winter months. It's not like you have to."

She was blowing into her gloves to warm her hands after refilling the water tank. "You sound like everyone else," she grinned. "'Why do you spend time up at that old barn when you don't have to?' I get it all the time."

She lifted the heavy black hose and swung it up on the first bracket attached to the breezeway ceiling. Then she maneuvered it along the inside wall, fitting it over the many support brackets and nails, pulled it tight around the corner post and finally, putting all her weight into it, stretched it to hook on the catch screwed into the half wall of the mulch hay bay. If the hose wasn't taut enough, it would surely freeze solid in the winter. She straightened up, caught her breath and continued, "And when I try to explain it … well, I can't." She put her hands on her hips and looked around the barn, her breath rising in plumes. "Like up there." She pointed to the barn ceiling. "I like to look up and see those big beams holding everything up. And the little window at the peak. The way the light comes through like it's sliding down a chute."

"I guess you've earned your hay in the bra," I said.

"I can't say I like *that*," she laughed with an involuntary hitch of her shoulders. "But when I change from my barn clothes and hay and shavings sift out on the floor it reminds me that I belong to this other place."

After the horses are let out, we watch them from the back door of the barn as they chase one another around the hay piles. Today, they won't settle down. Godiva runs Margie halfway out into the pasture. The other horses follow, skidding on ice, bucking and head tossing.

"Spring coming," I announce. Susan looks dubious. It's still in the single digits, though the light is lengthening. Steam rises from the manure pile at the east corner of the barn and the icicle fangs hanging from the eaves of the roof drip iridescent globes of light. Snow still covers the pasture, but under the surface, I can see—or feel—the paths beneath. Worn deep as faith.

OUTBITCHING THE MAESTRO

YOU CAN'T OUTBITCH the miserable, old son of a bitch, but on occasion I try.

Winter is prime bitching season and there couldn't have been a better day for it: five degrees with fits of wind following two days of snow and more coming. Only, it wasn't supposed to be winter anymore. It was early April, and the cruelty of this double-back of winter was enough to break the spirit. The old barn groaned with each smack of wind that pounded the doors, rattled the windows almost out of their panes, and sent snow sifting down from the ridgepole and blowing under the door and across the floorboards. Even Peter Twitch stayed hay mow bound, eschewing his usual duties as barn greeter.

Out of perversity of his own kind, the miserable old son of a bitch never cancelled a trimming due to weather. I figured if I must be there, I had bitching rights, so before he could settle on a theme, I had mine at the ready: boarders.

Of my many duties managing the Rumsley barn, chasing people down for overdue board payment is the least savory. Just that morning, Eve had met me at the barn with a repentant grin that said she had only excuses to offer. She was already two months behind, and Arvis had started grumbling about selling her horse, Margie, for back board. I knew he wouldn't, but Eve didn't.

"If I could jar excuses," I complained to the farrier's butt, "I'd feed the hungry." Eve's excuses, I knew by now, were consigned to her by an alcoholic husband, but I wasn't feeling particularly charitable. "He didn't get a paycheck, gambled away his paycheck, stole the money from her paycheck. And now she has to bail him out of jail! I could go on."

Boo straightened as best he could, turned with a weary sigh that said "please don't." Ozzy wore the same expression.

"People like that shouldn't have horses," he proclaimed. His face was fiery with cold. He wore canvas overalls but never hat or gloves. He swiped his sleeve across his face, leaving a long, thin proboscis of snot trailing from his beard. "They can't afford to take care of themselves let alone a thousand-pound animal." He walked around Ozzy, leaned back, squinted, and with a flick of his hand signaled that Ozzy was done. I brought Trixster out. He looked her over like he might send her back. "Do that woman a favor. Sell the damn horse."

The horses, anxious to get out to their piles of hay, were pawing the floor in their stalls, blowing opaque clouds of vapor in the frigid air. Their eyes glittered in the cold; frost coated the whiskers on their muzzles.

"You don't understand," I said to his butt again, but I didn't elaborate on what he didn't understand. It was more than he had time for. Judgments are convenient. Pre-packaged, no mixing required.

Over the year that Eve had been boarding her horse, Margie, at the farm, I had learned more and more about her "difficulties." She worked two exhausting, low-paying jobs—as a home aide for the most demanding, penurious old woman in Galway, and delivering papers, a job that required her to be up at two in the morning seven days a week. She had three half-grown children and an addicted and abusive husband. Sometimes they didn't have money for food or fuel oil. "She tries," I said at last. "She tries harder than anyone I know."

Eve often talked about her life in Michigan on her family's horse farm. It was a life she hoped to return to. Margie was foaled there. Eve trained her, rode her daily, and even showed her. Why she left and moved to

Upstate New York, she never made clear. She hasn't had a normal life since, she told me once in a moment of despair. But she hangs on hard to Margie and the belief that they will go home again.

"Horse people," the farrier snorts. He picks up the momentum I'd dropped and is already on his favorite topic: the bumptious, deluded, incompetent last customer. I'll make a good story for his next stop.

After the miserable old son of a bitch has gone, I let the horses out of the barn. They push by one another to claim a pile of hay. Finally, all six horses settle in and munch contentedly. I watch them for awhile from the back door of the barn.

This winter has been the hardest and longest in memory. There have been days when Arvis has called out to me "Thirty below." Cold that can kill. Thinking of it makes me question why I do this. What holds me so hard to this place? I think Eve would understand.

MUD SEASON

I USED TO CALL IT SHIT-STEW SEASON, which always drew a reprimand, along with a little guilty chuckle, from Marilyn.

Spring meanders in bedraggled with a winter hangover. With winter behind us, we face the ugly truth it's left behind. The barn never looks more on the verge of sinking—the gaps in the siding, the missing boards, nails pulling away from their seatings, the flaking paint revealing bare, weather-ravaged wood. Everything askew, exposed, depleted. The manure pile looms like a smoldering dragon on the east corner of the barn, and pyramids of manure and divots from hooves pockmark the pasture. The drip of melting snow from the roof valleys adds another desultory note.

Susan stands in her rubber boots shin-deep in tobacco-colored water, manure bobbing around her. She is trying to pick out the run-in shed, but doesn't know which to use—a manure fork, a shovel, or a bucket. The shit stew is deepest there due to Butch and Wally's spectacular roof repair failure of two summers ago. I wave on my way to fill the water tank. She only manages a weak smile. Her ebullience has gone flat. Mud season is a test.

Now that snow is off the ground, it's time to survey the fence line. I can see Arvis and I will have a lot of fencing to replace as several trees are down in the hedgerow at the far end of the front pasture. We should call Slovak right away, too, I remind myself, as there are not enough hay bales left for the cats to hide behind, and the pasture looks like it hasn't given grass a thought yet. I start to get a little dizzy with the mounting list of chores as I look around winter's battlefield.

Not to worry, I tell myself. Arvis is getting to it. Actually Arvis is occupied these days studying his nautical maps, preparing for his summer escape to Maine.

Amanda and Farrell, with Peter Twitch between them, are sitting atop the wellhouse trying to sketch the horses as they chase around the piles of hay. I am ever amazed at the friendship between Amanda and Farrell. Amanda has enticed Farrell out of her squeamishness over spiders, bats, and eating hedgerow apples. She has taught her the ways of horses and the knack of finding lost kittens. Farrell has taught Amanda the Zen of drawing.

There's not much Zen going on now though. The girls have abandoned drawing as the horses have gone spring crazy. The girls shriek and laugh and stomp their feet on the wellhouse roof as the horses spiral into spring mania. Godiva, the newest boarder, is chasing Cookie away from her pile of hay; Cookie chases Margie, who chases Angel, who chases Trixie. Ozzy just watches it all.

Tails up, the horses snort and squeal, backing their butts up to one another in kicking threats, then tearing off into the field, bucking and farting. They storm back, mud flying, Margie skidding in the mud, Godiva huffing a challenge; then, they parade around one another with tails high. Susan comes out of the run-in shed to see what all the commotion is about.

We all stand there watching the horses. The sun strengthens, the blackbirds string their calls from tree to tree, that busy, buzzy electricity that seems to plug spring into happening. The snow melt and recent rains have filled the well, and each time the pump kicks on the water gushes out with such energy the hose almost leaps out of the tank.

A jogger passes on Parkis Mills Road and stops. She waves and we all wave back with the enthusiasm of the winter freed. I know she must be admiring the barn. From there, none of its gaps are evident. It still looks like it will stand forever.

To the stacks of name plaques stored in the barn, I recently added Angel's.

Thanks, Angel, for all the years you took care of me and other clumsy riders, and for the adventures we shared.

And thanks for getting me into all this.

MARY CUFFE PEREZ is a writer of poetry, fiction, and nonfiction. She lives in the town of Galway, in Saratoga County, with her husband, Ken. *Barn Stories* is her fourth book and first work of creative nonfiction. She was born in Tennessee, and grew up in the Pacific Northwest before moving to New York. Much of her writing is inspired by the history, natural beauty, and people of rural upstate New York.